To J'
Merry Christn
love,
Barbie

BEYOND ALL REASON

BEYOND
ALL
REASON

My Life with Susan Smith

DAVID SMITH

WITH CAROL CALEF

KENSINGTON BOOKS

KENSINGTON BOOKS are published by

Kensington Publishing Corp.
850 Third Avenue
New York, NY 10022

Library of Congress Card Catalog Number: 95-077938
ISBN 0-8217-5220-0

First Printing: September, 1995

Printed in the United States of America

for Michael and Alex

A Personal Note

"I don't want to make one red cent off my two little boys."

I spoke those words to NBC interviewer Katie Couric in November 1994, a few short weeks after Michael and Alex had been taken from me. My whole life had just been ripped from its frame. I was shell-shocked and grieving, and missing my boys so much. When I told Katie I never wanted to sell my story to the tabloids, I meant it.

Some people might wonder if I'm betraying those words by writing a book. Deep in my heart I know the real reason I want to tell my story to the public, and it doesn't have a thing to do with dollars and cents.

What it has everything to do with is Michael and Alex, whose two young lives were ended in a horrible act of selfishness. As the weeks and months go by since they were murdered, I find myself more and more frustrated. Somehow, the focus has slipped away from them, the real victims in this terrible story.

When I hear the lawyers talking, when I hear them holding Susan Smith up as a "victim," it makes me angry. For myself, I would have rather stayed silent. But for Michael and Alex, I feel I have to speak.

By the time I heard my babies were gone, the murders had already been committed and there was nothing I or anyone could have done to save those children.

But because of Susan's lies, because she let them stay in the waters of John D. Long Lake for nine days, my sons' bodies were "totally ravaged." When they were recovered, the coroner had to recommend a closed coffin. So I never got to touch their little hands or kiss them one final time. I never got to say goodbye.

I know I'll never completely understand what has happened. But perhaps telling this story will help me to make peace with it all.

Nothing can ever approach the horror of what happened to Michael and Alex, of course, but some of the background leading up to it does not show human behavior at its best. I've left out the names of many of the people involved because I don't want to involve them personally in what is essentially my story and Susan's.

It was a crazy time. There are some things I regret now, a lot of behavior that looking back seems pretty immature. Could it be that somehow what Susan did was a product of all that catting around and foolishness and lying?

After Michael and Alex died, I got hate mail from people spitting out the venom. *If you had been a good husband and weren't out fornicating and stayed home with your wife, then your children wouldn't have been murdered . . .*

I tell myself over and over again that it can't be true.

People all over the world sneak around on each other, lie to each other, do each other dirt.

But no one kills their children. No one murders their babies.

You don't have to be guilty to feel guilty. If I could roll back the craziness, I would. I didn't have anything to do with the deaths of Michael and Alex, but if I could go back in time now and change things, I'd do it in a second. I would try harder to keep our lives on track. If it would just bring them back.

Nothing will accomplish that. All I can do today is what I think is right, in any way I know how.

Susan took my babies from me twice, once when she murdered them, and once when she lied about it. She may ask forgiveness of her parents, of the country, of her God, and they may choose to give it. But nobody's grief or sorrow or forgiveness will restore my boys to me.

So I have a simple message. Remember who lost their lives. That's the most important thing I want to remind everybody. It's why I want to speak out now.

MY SPECIAL THANKS

Thanks are due to a great many people who helped me prepare this book. Tiffany Moss has given great support to me for a long time now, and she has generously allowed me to use portions of her story in my own.

My father, David Smith, and my stepmother, Susan Smith, both provided their recollections of this difficult time, as did my uncle, Doug Smith, and his wife, Sharon Smith. Their memories helped fill in the blank spots of my own. Their love and guidance were the biggest contributions anyone could make.

My lawyer, J. Michael Turner, also provided material and recollections—but much more than that, he was a strong figure of support and guidance. I could not have made it without him. Marvin Chernoff and Libby Morgan and all the people at Chernoff/Silver Associates gave me immeasurable help with the press. My editors, co-writers, and publishers at Kensington shaped the material into a story and made the story into a book. The agent who represented this project, David Chalfant of TCA, guided me via long distance.

There are many more people to thank, including all the people across the country and the world who poured out their love and support for my boys, which meant so much to me and to all of us who were caught in this tragic situation. Every prayer, every letter, every gesture mattered. It all helped more than I can say.

CHAPTER

ONE

H ow does a father's worst nightmare begin?

For me, it all began with a phone call. It's funny how something so ordinary can suddenly shatter your life, but when I think back to that moment now, back to the last time when my life made any sense, what I remember is how *ordinary* it all was.

I was doing the most typical thing in the world for me—stocking shelves at Winn-Dixie, the supermarket where I work. I was hanging shelf tags on the disposable diapers. It's brain-numbing work, and your mind wanders.

I was thinking about my boys, Michael and Alex, because Michael, at three, was about ready to get out of diapers. Like a lot of parents, I was sort of mentally tallying how many Pampers I might have to change on him and on fourteen-month-old Alex before they would leave them behind completely.

The manager's voice came over the store's public address system. "David Smith, please pick up line two." It was a few minutes after nine P.M. on October 25, 1994.

I walked to the floral department and took the call

there—thinking it might be a customer, maybe, or a friend—never imagining something might have happened to Michael and Alex.

Susan came on the phone, crying, hysterical, jabbering.

"He's got the kids—he won't let me get the kids—David, he's got the kids!"

"Susan? Susan! Slow down, tell me what—who's got them?"

"David, David—I tried to get them and he's got the kids, and I don't know where they went!"

I felt panic rising in my throat. Susan was sobbing too much to speak. Another person, a woman, got on the line. She was pretty incoherent, too.

"Mister Smith? Your kids—I'm so sorry, but your kids were—your wife is okay, but she got carjacked, and he took the children. They've got the law looking for him. The sheriff is here. Your kids are gone."

Then she began crying. "The babies . . . your kids . . ."

"What—?" Begging her, pleading. "Please, what's going on?"

I could hear Susan wailing in the background. A man's voice came on the phone.

"David Smith? This is Sheriff Howard Wells."

"What's happening to my kids?"

"We're out here at the McClouds' house on Route 49. Your wife has informed us that she was carjacked at the Monarch Mill traffic light. The perpetrator left the scene with the car. The children were in it. Your wife is okay, but at this time the kids are still missing. Mr. Smith, I think you should come out here. Do you know where John D. Long Lake is?"

Why was this happening? Why was the sheriff asking me where some lake was?

"Yeah, I know where it is."

"The McCloud place is up the hill, off the highway. The house on the right, just before the turnoff to the lake."

After I hung up the phone, I went into overdrive. I ran out of the store with hardly any explanation at all.

There was one huge monster thought taking over my brain, and it didn't leave room for anything else. No emotions, no analysis, no second-guessing.

I have to get my boys back.

That was it. That was the only thing on my mind. It's a wonder I didn't have an accident, because I was doing everything without thinking. Running on automatic, I tore across the Winn-Dixie lot to my car. I raced out onto Route 176, turned onto Route 49, and sped through downtown Union.

I own a five-year-old Honda. I didn't think that old car could do 120 mph anymore, but it rose to the occasion on that trip out to the McClouds'. I made the fifteen miles in ten minutes. I was passing everyone in sight. No one was going to get in my way that night.

"Michael, Alex, oh, God . . ."

I was trying to make deals with Him. "If You allow them to be okay," I prayed, "if You keep Michael and Alex from being harmed, I will . . . I will . . . *do . . . any-thing* . . . I know I haven't led a perfect life, but I will do better. I will walk the straight-and-narrow. Just make them safe. Please, Lord—make them safe."

Just once on that agonizing drive did a stray thought come loose and float up into my mind.

How could this have happened?

Susan was being followed. I had made sure of that. Tiffany, my girlfriend, had been keeping tabs on her movements almost every minute of that whole evening.

How could she have been carjacked without someone seeing it?

I had never been to John D. Long Lake in my life, and didn't know the McCloud family at all. But someone was looking out for me during that drive, since I managed to pull right up to the house on my first try, without losing my way or backtracking.

The place stood out on that dark road. Every window in the house was lit up. A floodlight lit the grass around the yard. Parked in the driveway was the sheriff's car with its headlights on.

A man I didn't know—and who I later found out was Rick McCloud—met me on the deck. "I'm looking for Susan Smith," I said.

"She's in here."

When I walked in, Susan literally collapsed, falling to the floor in front of me, crying. I had to pick her up and carry her in my arms like a baby, easing her limp body onto the living room couch, comforting her.

"They'll find them," I told her, trying to hold my own panic down. "I know they're going to find them."

And at that moment, I felt an utter certainty that Michael and Alex were safe and were going to be returned to us.

Susan's mother, Linda, and her stepdad, Beverly Russell, arrived. People were crowding in from all over: Susan's longtime friend Donna Garner, Donna's parents,

Barb and Walt, and her boyfriend, Mitchell Sinclair. There got to be dozens of people there, friends and relatives, all in that stranger's house.

Slowly, in the McClouds' living room, the bits and pieces of Susan's story came together for me. Mostly, the details didn't come from Susan—she was too much of a basket case.

Sheriff Wells was the one who told me the story as he knew it. That evening, when Susan stopped her Mazda at a red light in Monarch, a little crossroads-and-mill suburb on Union's eastern fringe, she had both kids strapped into their carseats in the back. It was just a normal Tuesday night.

Suddenly, a black man opened the passenger door and sprang into the car. He held a handgun to Susan's side and ordered her to drive.

Terrified, Susan drove out into the countryside, down the winding two-lane Highway 49. The carjacker kept telling her not to look at him, she said. About ten miles from town, he directed her to stop the car in the middle of the road and get out, while he slid across into the driver's seat.

"Can't I take my kids?"

"I don't have time!" the guy said to her.

"Please," she begged him. He pushed her across the seat and out the door.

"Give me my babies!" she screamed.

"I won't hurt them," he said, and he drove off into the night.

"I love y'all," Susan said she shouted after our sons, as the guy left her there, standing in the middle of the road.

After I'd heard it, I didn't feel there was any room to do

anything except believe Susan—totally, completely, a hundred percent. She was in terrible pain. She'd just seen her children torn from her.

What I concentrated on that night at the McClouds' was aiding the search for my boys in any way I could. I felt it was my role to act as some sort of go-between for Susan—who was still in bad shape, not able to communicate much—and the police.

At one point, the sheriff needed to get the Mazda's license plate number to alert other law enforcement agencies to be on the lookout for the car. But Susan couldn't remember her tag number. So he radioed in her name to get the number.

Nothing came up. "What?" Susan said. "That car is registered."

I said, "Wait a minute, Susan. Your car plates are under Susan Vaughn"—her maiden name—"not Smith." The sheriff checked that name and the plates came up right away. I felt I needed to hold it together to help out at times like that.

Sheriff Wells had already started the search effort. He was talking to the highway patrol, asking them to put as many officers on duty that night as possible to help out. He talked to the folks at SLED—the South Carolina State Law Enforcement Department. The search people were meeting in the parking lot of the lake across the way—the closest large space to use as a gathering place.

Already a SLED helicopter was on its way, one specially equipped with a heat sensor. It would use infrared to pick up any signs of life in the dense forest below—whether the living thing was a deer or a rabbit. If the carjacker had parked the Mazda, the helicopter would be able to sense the heat off the engine. If my sons were on foot, the sensor would register their body heat.

The helicopter went all over the county that night. The sheriff knew that in a situation like this, a kidnapping, the sooner you moved, the better. Waiting until the next day could spell disaster. That's why the sheriff also immediately arranged to notify the newspapers and TV people, with the idea that word could get out by the following morning. We had to get people aware that this had happened so they would be looking for the boys.

I could hear that helicopter flying overhead all night long. In a way, the noise it made was scary. It reminded me just how bad the situation was—that they had to use the helicopter, because they hadn't found the kids yet. That they had to go to that extreme measure.

Yet it was comforting to hear the chopper up there. It told me that the law enforcement people were doing their jobs, and that the person who'd taken Michael and Alex was going to be apprehended. The noise bolstered my confidence. *They're going to get him,* I thought.

I even let my anger boil over privately a few times, in my mind. *If I ever get my hands on the guy . . .* I thought. I fantasized about being alone with him in a jail cell. *Just give me five minutes with him . . .*

Then I would be snapped back into reality. The boys were still missing. I would hug Susan and try to keep our spirits up.

Our kids would be returned to us that night, or by the next morning at the latest. I was sure of it.

CHAPTER

TWO

B y midnight there was still no word. The McCloud house was beginning to bulge at the seams. Susan's friends and family milled about. Sheriff Wells approached Susan and me to talk about the situation.

"We've got to let these folks get some rest," he said, meaning the McClouds. Their home was starting to resemble a police command post. "I need somewhere to reach you all."

Susan didn't hesitate. She just popped out with, "We'll be down at my mama's," and gave him the phone number.

I wasn't surprised. Home for Susan wasn't our home, the house on Toney Road that we had bought a year and a half before, midway through our marriage; it was her mama's house, the house she'd been raised in.

Sheriff Wells knew where she meant. The Russells were pretty prominent in Union. They lived out at Mount Vernon Estates, an uppity subdivision west of town. Sheriff Wells was good friends with Scotty Vaughan, Susan's brother, who lived in the same development, a few doors away. Wells and his wife were godparents to Scotty's two children.

Sheriff Wells himself actually lived just down Toney Road from us, across Route 176. Union is a close-knit town, where everybody knows your name, and everybody knows your business.

I wasn't crazy about Susan's choice of where to go that night. I had never had the best relationship with my in-laws.

"Don't you think we'd be better off at our house?" I asked her, meaning Toney Road.

"A lot of people might be coming by," she said, "and our house can't hold all of them."

I finally agreed. If Susan wanted to go home to her mama, I wasn't going to stand in the way. I knew she and her mother were close. I was ready to be there for her, wherever she was.

When Sheriff Wells saw us hugging and comforting each other that night, he assumed Susan and I were still happily married. But we were already separated and going through divorce proceedings.

What Sheriff Wells saw that night was not a husband and wife, but a father and mother, coming together out of concern for their kids. Susan was acting, but I wasn't. All our troubles, all our spats and not getting along—well, for me, it just blew straight out the window when I heard that Michael and Alex were in trouble.

Tragedy does that. It puts things in perspective. At that moment, I didn't care about all the problems between Susan and me. Nothing mattered except that our kids were lost. And we had to stick together to get them back.

It was about twelve-thirty when we left the McClouds'. I was still in my automatic mode, just "Do, do, do," focusing on where my next step would take me, all with the end in mind of getting this nightmare over with and getting my boys back.

As soon as we got out of the house, Susan calmed down a lot. We set off in my Honda—but not for the Russells', it turned out, not right away.

"I want to go to Toney Road," she said. "I have to get my contacts and some other things." I was glad to see Susan straighten up a little bit when we got away from the others. She was now less weepy.

"Okay," I said. "That's fine. We'll go get whatever you want."

She was wearing her glasses, and we knew we had to go down to the sheriff's department later that night. I thought that maybe she preferred to talk with the officers there while wearing her contact lenses. I wasn't going to fuss at her about it.

The darkness closed in around the car as soon as we got away from the blaze of lights at the McClouds'. We headed back toward Union on Route 49. There were a lot of creeks and fishing holes along that road, and I kept a lookout on all the bridges, thinking I might see the burgundy Mazda abandoned down one of the embankments.

All the while I kept dogging Susan, questioning her, hoping I might jog loose some memory that could be useful.

"Well, where did he let you out?"

"Right back there."

"Were there any other cars around?"

"I don't remember. No."

We were silent for a little while. I kept being flooded with panics and fears, trying to push them back, keep them out of my head, since I didn't think I'd be much use to anyone if I fell apart. Every car that passed I burned with my eyes, looking for that Mazda.

Susan wasn't crying at all now. She was calm. I was snapping a lot of questions at her, still trying to get more details that would help the search.

Then she said something strange. "Listen," she said. "Tom Findlay might come and see me. If he comes down, you can't get mad or anything. I don't want you two to get into a fight."

That floored me. Tom Findlay was Susan's boyfriend. She'd been seeing him ever since we'd separated, even before. I chalked the comment up to the differences between Susan and me. My sons had just disappeared and she was telling me not to get upset over a visit by some man she was seeing?

"Susan, I don't give a damn who visits," I said, trying to keep my voice even. "I'm worried about those kids. I don't care if Tom Findlay comes over. I don't care if the President of the United States comes to call. I just want to get those boys back."

"I do, too," she said quickly. "I miss them so much."

We reached the outskirts of Union. "Where exactly did it happen?" I asked Susan.

"Right here. The red light."

The Monarch Highway intersection, where Susan said she had gotten carjacked, was the first light we hit on our way to town. There was a big old mill hulking off to the left, and a church to the right, but there weren't many cars that late at night. I slowed down and crept through the crossroads.

I asked her all sorts of questions. Which direction did the guy come from? Was there anyone else on the street? How long had she been stopped? I wanted to know everything, but getting more details from Susan was like pulling teeth.

All she could give me was the same basic outline, over and over again. It was frustrating.

So I drove on, through downtown Union, then up past Hardee's and the football field and Wal-Mart and Winn-Dixie, all the familiar landmarks of our lives together, to the house we owned on Toney Road.

Here was the place where my kids had grown up. They had run crazy laughing through this yard, played outside in the fenced-off carport, gone crying to their mama when they fell down and skinned their knees. This was their home.

We got out of the car and went inside. On the surface, I was still in my do, do, do mode—pick up the things Susan needs, call Mom, do this, do that. But underneath, my emotions were all riled up.

Just walking through the door of that house was a tremendous relief. It was just how Susan and the boys had left it earlier that night. All of Michael's and Alex's things were there. The house was filled with toys and photos, tiny sneakers and sweatshirts hung up by the door. The place still seemed warm from those boys' touch, and it made me feel a lot better that night.

I called my mother and told her what had happened. When I got off the phone, Susan was still getting her things together. I straightened the house up a little. I picked up some toys, cleaned a few dishes off the counters in the kitchen, and washed the children's plates and spoons.

I figured they'd have the kids back within hours, maybe even sooner. It struck me as impossible that the boys would not be back to fill those rooms with life. It looked like they had just stepped out, as if they were maybe out back, playing in the yard . . .

I still had my faith telling me that God would take care of them, wherever they were. I thought they were out there, that we hadn't found them yet, but that they were okay. He would watch over them. Walking into those rooms so filled with the boys' spirit just verified that for me.

With Susan in the bathroom getting her contacts, I allowed myself a moment, just a moment, to be alone with Michael and Alex. I let my memories of the boys rush over me.

When had I last seen them?

It was three days earlier, the previous Sunday. The boys were visiting my apartment. We'd do the same stuff we usually enjoyed. They were playing with their toys, and I chased them around the place and rode them on my back.

The clearest memory I have is the silly little children's game they were playing with a set of blocks. Michael would pile them up in a grand tower, and Alex would come plowing through like a steamroller, knocking down whatever Michael had built. Alex would chuckle and then that would start Michael laughing, too. Alex had a cute little laugh you could catch like spring fever.

That day was the kind of calm, happy family time we

tried to spend together often. Even though Susan and I had been separated three months, since that August, even though we were going through a divorce, we were still raising Michael and Alex together, as a regular mother-and-father team. My new apartment was only about five minutes from our old place on Toney Road.

Susan and I didn't have any formal custody agreement, just a loose understanding that it would be a good thing for the boys to see their father as much as possible. We both wanted for me to be as close to them as I had always been.

When at the end of the day I would bring Michael and Alex home to Susan at Toney Road, I'd stay a while, getting them ready for bed. I'd give Michael a bath—he loved his bath, but hated getting his hair washed.

We'd put Alex to sleep in his crib, each one of us kissing him and saying goodnight. Afterward, the three of us—Susan, Michael, and I—would make a pallet on the floor, and we'd all lie down together until Michael went to sleep.

It was an odd situation, being stretched out in the dark next to my estranged wife, but it was all for the boys. Ever since Michael was born, he had slept in bed with Susan and me, and he'd grown accustomed to falling asleep between us. We were trying to make the best of it for Michael and Alex, trying to give them at least some semblance of a family life.

A lot of my motivation for staying on good terms with Susan came from not wanting to be apart from Michael and Alex, not wanting to be shoved out of their life. I never wanted the divorce—that was Susan's idea. If she changed her mind, I was ready to try to work it out with her.

I was seeing the boys develop day by day and just loving

them more and more. Anyone who knows kids knows that by the time they reach Michael's age of three, they've already formed pretty complete little personalities.

"Mike-Mike" we called him, and Alex was always "Fat Rat." Michael was the type of kid who got his feelings bruised easily. A sensitive boy. He loved to play, he was very active, but if you said "Boo!" to Michael, in no time that lower lip would poke out and start quivering.

Alex was different. Nothing bothered him much. But Fat Rat was the baby, and his big brother Michael was very protective of him.

If we were out in the yard at Toney Road and I was busy doing some chore, fixing the lawn mower, say, and Alex began to wander off, Michael would say something like, "Daddy, where's Alex going?" Not to tattle on him, but to let me know that Alex might be getting in trouble.

At the nursery, if one of the older kids took something away from Alex, Michael would get that toy back for his baby brother right quick. He would stand up for Alex. Even when Alex bopped Michael on the head or pulled his hair, Michael wouldn't lash out at him.

One time, a neighbor's cat came into the backyard at our Toney Road house. Alex was playing, chasing the cat, and the cat was running away from him. Then suddenly the cat stopped, and Alex stopped, and the cat started running again—but this time it was headed right toward Alex. Alex took off running the other way, just scared to death. But Michael came down across the backyard after that cat, protecting his brother. Michael would have chased that cat clean to Mississippi.

Michael was getting to be a big talker. He could carry on

a conversation just like you and me. He enjoyed books. He'd love me to read to him, and talk about the pictures. Especially the Snoopy comic strip.

Michael was happiest outdoors. He liked to work with tools, to "help" me in my shop in the carport. I was raised to fix things myself when I could, rather than taking something out to get it fixed. While I worked, Michael would take a little wrench and just fiddle with it. Anything I was doing, he wanted to help. Even if it was just tying up the trash, he'd want to have his little hands in there, trying to tie the bag up, too.

Michael and I were close. He was a daddy's boy. Susan told me that when I wasn't living at home, Michael would wake up in the middle of the night, crying: "I want my Da-da." I only kept Michael for sleepovers at my apartment a few times, but when I did, he never woke up at night, wanting Susan or crying for her. He was fine as long as he was with his daddy.

Alex was still a baby and more attached to his mama. I was working on him, trying to bring him around to being a daddy's boy, too. But I was close to both my sons. I'd feed Alex his baby food. If either child was sick at night, I'd get up with him, sometimes before Susan would, and rock him back to sleep.

I did for those kids. I'll plead guilty to being a lousy husband to Susan. But I was a good father to Michael and Alex.

When Susan and I left Toney Road after picking up her contact lenses, it was around two A.M. We headed toward the Russells'. But Susan wanted to make another stop.

"Let's go get some drinks and stuff," she said. We were driving down Route 176, the Duncan Bypass four-lane, to the west of downtown. It was the big commercial strip where pretty much all the businesses of Union had relocated. We were passing Winn-Dixie and Susan was suggesting we stop in.

This isn't quite as strange as it sounds. I know—your kids are missing and you're thinking about going shopping? But you have to understand the place that Winn-Dixie held in our lives. It was central, not just because we had both worked there, but because it was so much the focus of the town, too.

Winn-Dixie was in a good-sized shopping mall, with the town's Wal-Mart at the other end and a McDonald's in the middle of the parking lot. It was the place where a lot of the people just naturally hung around, especially the kids. The authorities had closed the parking lot of the high school football field across the street because kids were getting too rowdy, breaking bottles and getting into fights. The action then just transferred to the mall parking lot.

Every night, there'd be people parked there, talking to each other or cruising through the lot, slowing down for the speed bumps and shouting hello to someone they knew. The town fathers might disapprove of it all, but there was nowhere else for kids to go. There was nothing else going on in Union.

So to drive down Route 176 and turn into Winn-Dixie was part of our routine. We headed toward the store and right away I noticed that Tiffany's car was parked there. I could see that she was still sitting in the car, probably wondering what was going on.

Tiffany knew some of it, because I had called the store earlier, from the McClouds'. I had spoken with Nicole, a woman I worked with and a friend of Tiffany's. I asked if she could please get the extra set of keys I kept at the store, drive to my apartment, and get my father's phone number in California. I wanted my dad to be notified about what had happened.

Nicole and Tiffany both drove over to the apartment. Tiffany had met my father a few times before and called him.

"Are you sitting down?" she asked.

"What's the matter with David?" my dad said.

"It's not David. Somebody's kidnapped Michael and Alex. They jumped in Susan's car."

She told him what little she knew: that as crazy as it sounded, the boys had been taken by a stranger who'd stolen Susan's car.

Before he got off the phone, my dad reassured Tiffany: "This person couldn't have just appeared in Union. Somebody's got to know him. They'll have him by morning." My dad knew that a stranger in Union would stick out like a sore thumb.

When I saw Tiffany at Winn-Dixie, I wanted to go over to her and talk, but I couldn't. It was almost as if I'd become another person. I couldn't see making Susan's situation more difficult than it already was. I know just walking past like that hurt Tiffany, but I wasn't thinking about her. Right then, my place was with Susan, and that's all there was to it.

It was after hours, and the Winn-Dixie was locked, but there were a few people inside, doing the stocking. As assistant manager, I had a set of keys. The news that something had happened to our boys had traveled through the store—and through the town itself—pretty fast. These people were our extended family, and it was good to hear all their expressions of support and concern. Somehow, though, I ended up reassuring them more than they comforted me.

CHAPTER

THREE

Winn-Dixie is my own special world.

I started working there the month after I turned sixteen, in August 1986, putting in twenty or twenty-five hours a week. It's an excellent company because they treat their employees well and the mood in the store is pretty light and upbeat. Sometimes it got to be like a supermarket soap opera, with all the flirting and dating and gossiping that went on. But mostly it was like a family with seventy-five members who liked each other and wanted to help.

I couldn't always say the same for my own family.

When I was two, my folks moved from Royal Oaks, Michigan, where I was born, down to Union, near my mother's childhood home out in the country. Soon after we got settled, a few Jehovah's Witnesses came to call on my mom. Our home life was never the same after that.

It is hard for a little kid to understand religion. What I did realize was that our family had to act differently from other families because we were ''JWs.'' And I had a sharp understanding of all the ''no's'' that my mother was always laying on the rest of us. No movies. No dancing. No celebration of holidays or birthdays. I wasn't even allowed to play sports in school.

I guess I've made my peace with it now, but I was bitter about it when I was young. We received a lot of teasing from the other kids. There was no way I could get my mother to realize how uncomfortable it made me and my brother Danny feel, coming up in high school and going around from door to door, as is required by the Jehovah's Witness teachings, preaching about the Bible. Sometimes I'd knock on a door and a classmate of mine would answer, and I'd just about die from embarrassment.

It made me feel bad, too, when after Christmas the other kids would come back to school with their new clothes and gifts, talking about how their daddy and mama had bought them this or that, while all we had were hand-me-downs and homemade toys. The Jehovah's Witnesses are strict in being against all celebrations of holidays, so we were totally cut out from the whole mood of Christmas.

Even the cards and presents we got from Dad's folks up in Michigan were intercepted by my mother, torn up, and destroyed. All we knew about them was their names.

My parents had a rocky marriage, but my father made do by throwing himself into his work. When I was in high school, he held down two full-time jobs—as a mechanic for the City of Union, and as a meter reader—and ran a cleaning service in his spare time. He went by the name David, though his name was Charles David. Since I loved the Winnie-the-Pooh stories as a kid, my family nicknamed me the "Bear" so no one got Dad and me confused.

I had a father who was often gone at work, and a mother

who was hauling us down to the Kingdom Hall every Saturday and oftentimes during the week, too. Danny and I would try to get out of going to the Hall by working for our dad. In a way, I guess that's sort of what instilled in me a strong work ethic.

By the time I turned seventeen, the tensions between my mother and me had boiled over to where I could not stay at home. I was in the process of rejecting the Jehovah's Witnesses and turning my faith toward more mainstream Methodist teachings. Also, like any normal, hot-blooded teenage boy, I wanted to begin dating.

My mother wouldn't hear of anyone living under her roof who wasn't under her thumb. The least little thing would set us off. If she said, "Load the dishwasher," and I didn't jump up and do it right then, that would start an argument. It got to where she would even lash out, swatting me a couple of times. We were like a powder keg ready to explode.

So, I finally told her I was moving out.

"Fine, you can move out," she told me. "But if you do, that means no more meals, no more school clothes, no more nothing from us. You move out and you're on your own."

"That's fine by me," I said, talking big. And I stormed out.

I didn't have to go far, though. My mother's grandmother, my great-grandmother, lived about fifty yards down the road in an old country-style home surrounded by lilac trees and vegetable gardens. She was a good, generous lady named Forest Malone, but all her grandchildren and great-grandchildren called her "Moner." She took me into her house, no questions asked. It helped that my brother Danny was already living there with her.

I knew I could take care of myself partly because I was working at Winn-Dixie. My grades came down a lot because I was working so much, but it made me feel good to pay my own way.

I wasn't bitter or resentful about it. I was proud of what I was doing. Go to school, go to work, go to sleep; get up and do it all over again. When graduation came, I paid for my own cap and gown.

One thing that taking home a paycheck did was make me think I was more mature than I probably was. I bought my own clothes, bought furniture for my room at Moner's, and took care of myself in every way. I was working as an adult, paying taxes—who was going to tell me I was still just a kid?

I lost my virginity during that first year of freedom, to a girl I'd met in school the spring before. I'd spent time with girls, of course, at the local skating rink or at church activities, and I'd done my share of sneaking off to the woods to mess around. But I'd never yet done any real dating, which in my mom's eyes was strictly forbidden.

This girl had seen my picture in my eleventh-grade yearbook and asked one of her friends to deliver a letter she'd written me. When she started calling my house over the summer, it was when the frictions had just gotten really bad between my mother and me, and my falling for a girl was the last straw. I moved to Moner's and started dating the girl for real.

My first girlfriend had big brown eyes and had a reputation as a get-around girl. It made me mad when people would talk bad about her. It was wintertime, and I would bundle up and take my motorcycle over to her house, and then we'd take her mother's car and hang out at the high school football field, or go out for a burger.

We dated for two months. After the first month we had sex for the first time, on a dirt road, in the back of a car. We'd done it a total of maybe five times when she told me she was pregnant. I was seventeen and scared to death.

My girlfriend called me up one morning and said, "I ain't going to go to school today."

"Ain't going to school?" I said. "Why not?"

She said, "I'm going to have an abortion."

The news totally floored me. I said, "Do what?"

"My mom wants me to," she said. And that was it. I was upset, partly because I'm not for abortions, except if it's a rape or something like that. But mainly, I was young and naive and stupid, and I believed, even as a twelfth grader, that I was ready to take care of a child.

"Just have the baby," I said. "Please. Give him to me. I'll take him and raise him and pay for everything."

I begged her to reconsider, but it was a done deal. She and her mother had scheduled a doctor's appointment without even consulting me. I was powerless to prevent what I thought of as an awful tragedy.

It was pretty arrogant of me to think I could take care of a kid at that age. Later on, I would realize what an immense responsibility babies are, and how emotionally compli- cated parenthood can be. But back then, I thought I could manage it.

When my girlfriend went ahead and had the abortion, it ended our relationship.

In my social life I started to move away from the high school crowd and get more involved with people I met at work. Soon after I stopped seeing my first girlfriend, I met the girl to whom I eventually got engaged. I'd known her since we'd gone to junior high. When I was a senior, she became a cashier at Winn-Dixie. This girl was about as nice as you could imagine. She was fun and easy to be around, she was sweet and polite, she cared about others, and she was very good at relating to people. She did well in high school, got good grades, and was talking about attending college when she graduated.

I never knew for sure why she was so eager to get married, but I suspected she was trying to escape her life at home. She had terrible arguments with her parents and would call me, crying, at three in the morning, desperate. Part of the reason I dated her as long as I did was because I felt like I was her only shield from her family.

I even fixed up the house down the road from my parents' place for after we were married, and put $6,000 into redoing the inside and fixing the roof.

But all the time, I was just going through the motions. I was going to marry this girl because it was what she wanted. I was going to wreck my life, marry someone I didn't love, to make her happy.

Deep down inside, there was a tiny voice telling me that one way or another, I was going to get out of it. I was not going to get married. It sounds cold, me leading her on like that, letting her plan a wedding and everything, if I knew I wasn't going through with it. All I can say is that I was young and not that good at communicating my feelings.

I first really got to know Susan in the summer of 1988, when she came to work as a cashier at Winn-Dixie in the summer between her junior and senior years of high school. I had just graduated.

Union's high school is small, and Susan had been a grade behind me, so of course I always knew of her, in a vague sort of way. The closest I ever got to her, before she started working alongside me, was that my older brother Danny knew her high school boyfriend real well. Danny would always joke about Susan with the guy.

"Hey, you've got to get her to wear those short skirts to school." Then Danny would laugh, to make sure the guy would know he didn't mean any disrespect. It became a running joke between them. Danny always liked Susan, though—and she always caught my eye, too, when I saw her passing in the halls.

I remember the first time I really got a good look at Susan. It was in the store. She was surrounded by three or four guys. They were from high school, younger than she was, and they were all laughing and making small talk as she checked through their purchases. The bagger was laughing along with them.

For a long time, I'd watched Susan from a distance. We had only the briefest of conversations. Then I started bagging her groceries and we just kind of started talking. A little later on, I started to make it a point to pass by her register.

Right away she struck me as an attractive girl. Susan had

a million-dollar smile. She had pretty hair. She had a bigger chest than girls I had gone out with before, and that was attractive to me. In the summer, Susan would always lay out in the sun for hours to get a real dark tan.

She didn't wear real short skirts. She would never wear tight Spandex biker shorts or anything like that. It wasn't her style. In high school, she usually went out with preppy-style guys. She always dressed very conservatively, very nice. She was a beautiful young woman and she knew it.

Even though she was all smiles, especially to men, I wouldn't have called Susan a flirt. If a guy she didn't know well came up to her, she would never hug his neck or kiss him on the cheek. She would just be bubbly: "Hey, how are you?" I think it would be easy to take her wrong; it would be easy to take her as being flirtatious. But she just had an extroverted, outgoing personality.

She turned heads, and she always felt confident about her appearance. What a guy would see when he looked at her—what I saw, the first time I really had a chance to check her out in Winn-Dixie—was someone who was more or less a hunk of hell, and knew it.

But there were one or two problems with Susan and me getting together at that point in our lives. One was that I was already seeing someone—someone I was supposed to be serious about, someone I was actually engaged to. When I started getting to know Susan, I had been dating my fiancée steadily for about two years. We had even set a date for an October wedding—almost a year away at the time.

The other problem was that just then Susan had a pretty complex romantic life of her own. As soon as she started in at Winn-Dixie, I began hearing rumors about her affairs with people who worked there.

People said she was seeing not one but two of her co-workers. One of them I knew to be a married man. I couldn't figure it out, because he wasn't the best-looking guy. People who worked with him used to make fun of the way he talked. I couldn't imagine this guy with pretty, outgoing Susan Leigh Vaughan, who could easily get any man she wanted. But the rumors persisted.

Everyone talked about Susan at that store, the stockboys and baggers and clerks. People would notice the way she and this guy hung all over each other all the time, were always huddled up together, talking, how they stayed in the office late at night after the store closed. If he got a call on the pay phone outside his office when Susan happened to be off work, it was likely that Susan was calling him.

Everyone knew they were seeing each other. But pretty soon people were talking about another co-worker who was also a good deal older than Susan.

During Susan's second summer at the store, once she'd gotten out of high school, she would tell her mama she was working the third shift at another job she had in town, when she was actually spending the night with this older beau.

I didn't know what to think about all this. I didn't like hearing people laugh behind Susan's back. They'd talk about her, run her down a lot. Susan was a "slut" or a "whore," dating a married man who was old enough to be her father, and sneaking around behind his back with someone else. I began to feel sorry for her. It degraded her, all the gossip.

Eventually, Susan's affairs all came to an end. One man maneuvered to have his competition transferred to another Winn-Dixie in another county (if he could have had him packed off to Nome, Alaska, he would probably have done it).

Then he began to see his marriage fall apart on account of what he was doing with Susan. His wife and kids came into the store one time when Susan was working, and his wife said, "I see your baby's working tonight." She wasn't stupid. On her days off, Susan had been driving clear to the next county to this guy's house. His wife was always out at her job.

He knew his wife would divorce him if he didn't do something. That was when he requested a transfer out of Union to another Winn-Dixie and told Susan it was over between them.

And Susan attempted suicide.

"Attempted suicide" sounds serious, but what Susan really did was swallow a nonlethal dose of Anacin. The news spread through the store like wildfire. Susan had to go up to Spartanburg Regional Medical Center for a few days, then she took a month off from work.

When she returned, things settled down some. The two men she'd been with were gone. At the same time, the girl I was engaged to left her Winn-Dixie cashier job for another job in town. It seemed that things were working out to clear the field for Susan and me.

CHAPTER

FOUR

I remember getting out of the car in front of the Russells' big three-bedroom ranch house with the soft drinks and doughnuts we'd brought from Winn-Dixie and taking a deep breath. It was two o'clock Wednesday morning and every light in the place was on. I didn't feel tired at all. But Susan was exhausted.

Bev Russell met us at the front door. I desperately wanted him to tell me that there was some sort of good news, but all he did was grab us both in a big hug and say, "We're praying for them."

By Union standards, Beverly and Linda Russell were important people. Bev had come from money. He was the nephew of Donald Russell, a former governor of the state. He ran a successful investment and tax consulting business and at one time owned a big appliance store in town. Susan was around seven years old when her mother, Linda Sue, married Bev. Harry Ray Vaughan, Susan's natural father, had killed himself a short time after his divorce from Linda had become final.

Bev was a church man, active in the Christian Coalition,

and he was big on prayer. My father sometimes called Bev
"Thank you, Jesus" instead of his name. I usually went
along with Bev's prayer circles, but I couldn't help being a
little repelled by what I felt was the hypocrisy of the man.

A couple of years earlier, Susan had confessed to me
that her stepdad had molested her.

We'd been lying in bed, and I'd been opening up to her
about troubles I'd had in my family. Suddenly she said,
"There's something you need know, too." And she told
me what Beverly had done to her.

It had happened a few years before, Susan told me. More
than a few nights, her stepfather would come into her bedroom late, while she was sleeping. He used to fondle her
breasts and put her hand on his genitals.

Susan told me she pretended to be asleep and rolled over
on the other side of the bed to get away from him. But he
just got up and walked around the bed and started doing it
to her again.

"Then he started up open-mouth kissing me," Susan
said.

"How could you pretend to be asleep when he was
Frenching you?" I asked her.

"I just did," she said. That sort of made sense to me at
the time. I figured it was a typical thing to do in that situation, because you're scared and you don't know what to
do, so you just act like you're asleep.

It was a hard thing for her to live with. And, according to
Susan, it was even harder for her to tell Linda about it.
Things got so bad that Susan finally broke down and told
her school guidance counselor. Almost immediately, Linda
and Social Services got involved and so did the police.

Consumed with guilt, Beverly admitted that he had molested Susan.

But Linda and Susan never pressed charges. The court sealed the case records and required Bev, Linda and Susan to go for family counseling together up in Spartanburg. Susan said the counseling helped, but things weren't the same in the Russell home for a long time after that.

I never could look at Bev Russell in quite the same way again after Susan first told me about her troubles with him.

Bev probably couldn't look at me the same way, either, since he knew that I knew. He once asked Susan if she had told me everything, and she wasn't going to lie to him. She said that she had told me. Of course, he and I never spoke openly about it. That wasn't the way things were done around that household.

In those early-morning hours just after word began to get out that our boys were missing, friends and relatives were already holding vigil at the Russell house. But we couldn't stay. As soon as we set down our groceries, we were off again to downtown Union.

The sheriff wanted us to give him some information to help in the search for the boys. The first thing he needed was a detailed physical description of the carjacker so the police artist could come up with a sketch. That was fine with me, even though I could see that Susan was pretty exhausted emotionally. We got right back into the Honda and drove downtown.

I got blindsided when we went into the sheriff's office that first time. I guess I was kind of naive. I knew I had nothing to do with the disappearance of my sons, but the police had to find that out for themselves.

I had never been in trouble with the law. Not once, not when I was a kid, not later, when I grew up. But here we were in the old stone sheriff's headquarters—it looked like a military fort—in the middle of a cold, dark night, and I was being suspected of the most terrible thing in the world.

As soon as I walked into that station, they wanted to talk to "the husband, David Smith." They separated Susan and me. She was in a back room, and before I left, I saw the sheriff's deputies comforting her and bringing her coffee. I was led to another room and to be questioned.

Sheriff Wells and another deputy asked me where I was earlier that evening. But what really turned up the heat was when I told Sheriff Wells that Susan and I were having marital troubles.

"Well, it's no secret that we're going through a separation and a divorce and everything," I told him.

"I didn't know any of that," Sheriff Wells said. "When I saw you hugging and all out at the McClouds', I just naturally thought everything was okay."

"No," I told him. "We're in court for a divorce."

They started to hammer me then. "How come you're so calm?" the deputy demanded. "If it was me, if it was my kids missing, I would be on the floor wailing."

"People just react in different ways," I said. I didn't know how to explain to him that somewhere in my heart, I *was* on the floor wailing. But I was holding it together for the sake of Michael and Alex.

They were hounding the hell out of me, though. "Where

are your kids? You know where they're at. Where are they?''

And all the time I was thinking, *I've got nothing to do with this. Susan's got nothing to do with this. Just find Michael and Alex!*

When I told them I had been at Winn-Dixie all evening and had lots of witnesses to prove it, that took the heat off a bit. At about five o'clock in the morning they finally let up on me. I told them that of course I'd take a polygraph. They informed me they wanted Susan to take one, too.

"We'll take lie detector tests or anything else you want us to," I said, "but you'd best be out there looking for that car."

The bad blood between Sheriff Wells and me probably started right there. He's a good man and a good police officer, but the fifth degree he gave me that morning didn't sit right with me. It was frustrating and humiliating.

Sheriff Wells never apologized for sweating me, so later on, when he made what I thought were a couple of real insensitive moves, maybe I was all set to bear a grudge against him. All I know is that if you're in a job which requires you to deal with people who are out of their minds with grief and anxiety, you should learn how to go slow. Sheriff Wells just bulled through my emotions as if they weren't there.

Of course, in my rational mind, I wanted to cooperate in any way with the investigation into my sons' disappearance, but I just felt questioning and polygraphing us was a big waste of time. Sitting there, seeing them go after the wrong man, made the panic start welling up inside me. *Just find my boys!* I wanted to shout at them. I had a sense that time was going down the drain.

CHAPTER

FIVE

S usan dropped off to sleep on the couch as the sun came up on Wednesday, October 26. We hadn't returned from the sheriff's until nearly dawn. Susan was so tired, all she wanted to do was sit down. I was always up pacing, but she was always sitting down. I remember her in a chair, slowly sipping a cup of tea early that morning. Finally, she said she needed something to help her rest, and her family pharmacist rushed over a bottle of sedatives.

I couldn't imagine laying my head down; I was way too fired up. Instead, I paced the floor beside Susan, with the events of the night going around and around in my mind like a horrible dream. Aside from Susan, the house was full of activity. Everybody was up. Whenever the phone rang, we would all jump.

I remembered the few other times the boys had been in trouble. Once Michael was real sick. He caught a virus and spiked a fever. The poor little guy was only a year and a half old, and he was burning up. In the middle of the night, we took him up to Mary Black Hospital in Spartanburg.

"He's lost a lot of fluid," the nurse there told us. Both

of us stayed the night while they did everything to bring our baby's temperature down. For a week Michael had to stay in the hospital, getting fluids with an IV in his foot. I remember he couldn't walk, and we had to pull him around the corridors in a little wagon.

Later, the doctor said if his fever had stayed so high a couple more hours, Michael might not have made it.

I remember how the idea of losing Michael had sent me into the absolute depths of despair. But afterward, Michael's scary fever was just one of those childhood incidents that you look back upon and tell stories about: "Whew, that was a close call."

That Wednesday, after the disappearance, as I walked the floor next to Susan and listened to her breathe during her heavy, sedated sleep, my love for the boys translated itself into an overwhelming love for her. I wanted so much to protect her, to shield her from all the hurt I thought she was feeling.

I had never been totally convinced that she and I should divorce, anyway. She had wanted to, and she was so determined that I'd finally gone along with the idea. I loved her so much at that moment I thought I was going to be crushed by the power of my emotion.

It was us against the big bad world, and I swore to myself that there was no way the world was going to win. It was not going to take our boys from us. No one on the outside could know how Susan and I were feeling. Anything that was said against one of us was said against the other.

To give myself some solace in those hours when I couldn't sleep, I thought about the good times between Susan and me. I thought about the sugary sweet beginning of our relationship together, when she'd seemed like the most exciting woman in the world.

I thought about the strawberry kiss.

In the late summer of 1990, Susan and I started talking more, goofing around, out-and-out flirting with each other. I'd go up to the front cash registers to bag groceries. As I helped one of her customers we'd pass a few words, talk some trash to each other. Sometimes it seemed when I saw her there was an electrical charge that ran through me. She was so cheerful and smiling all the time, it made me feel good.

One evening, I was in the back stockroom of the store, working at a stainless steel sink. I trimmed some cabbage and then started wrapping corn in plastic wrap. I was alone, and Susan came back there to take her break with me. She had a drink and was eating some strawberries she had gotten out of produce.

She was nineteen years old, pretty and fresh as peaches, and she struck me as every bit as luscious as one of those berries she was eating. For the life of me, I can't remember what sort of small talk we made that night. But I do know that suddenly we stopped. For no reason at all, we stopped talking and looked at each other like we knew what was going to happen.

Then I kissed her. Our first kiss was a deep, long, open-mouthed kiss . . . full of strawberries. We laughed about it right afterward, when I backed away from her and pretended to pick strawberry seeds out of my mouth. It was wonderful.

We began seeing each other a short time later. And on

the second date, we had sex for the first time on the living-room floor at Moner's house after she'd gone to sleep.

Susan and I always had a good time. We were typical teenagers: we couldn't stand to be apart, always on the phone, calling each other. We'd drive twenty-five miles to Spartanburg to go to the movies (there are no movies in Union), or just go out to eat. She'd write me in a letter, "I'll love you forever."

Susan was different from the other girls I'd been with. With her, sex was relaxed and fun. She'd do sexy things like surprise me with a special black nightie that she'd wear under her everyday clothes.

I liked her and we had a lot of fun together. We both enjoyed sex. But there was no feeling on my part that we were going to get engaged or anything like that. I saw my-self with Susan as just catting around—nothing serious. After all, I still was engaged to another girl.

Susan and I weren't too regular about using protection. Partly, it was because one of the men Susan was with before me had a medical problem that made it impossible for him to get a woman pregnant. So, Susan was used to not taking precautions and, in the heat of the moment, I went along.

A few months later, all that changed. Susan came up to me at work and told me that her period was late.

Those are not exactly the words a guy wants to hear from a girl he's sneaking around with behind his fiancée's back. We hadn't been together for long. She was nineteen and I was twenty.

I didn't worry about it too much right then. I thought it

might be a false alarm. We waited every day for a week for Susan's period to start, but it never did. Still, I figured she was just irregular; it was no big deal. I spent a lot of time sitting in the break room at the store, praying that Susan would get her period.

Oh God, please don't let her be pregnant.

Then Susan brought one of those over-the-counter early pregnancy tests to work. She took the test in the Winn-Dixie staff bathroom, and I waited upstairs in the break room for her to come out. When she did, she showed me the results—a little blue dot in a plastic sleeve.

I just shook my head and said, "Oh, hell."

We sat down together at one of the picnic tables the store had up there. We were alone, and we just grabbed each other's hands and prayed out loud. "Lord, please give us some direction, some guidance on what to do now."

I was happy I was going to be a father. At that time I thought I was ready for a child. It was a shock, but I was happy.

I also knew I had some tough scrambling to do to sort out everything that had just gotten confused by Susan's being pregnant.

The day I found out I was going to be a father, I called my fiancée to tell her about Susan and me. I said hello and started to cry.

"What's the matter?" she said.

I just laid it on her. "Susan's pregnant."

Her world came crumbling down. "Why did you sleep with her? Why didn't you tell me you were seeing her?"

We stopped communicating almost from that second on. We talked a few more times on the phone, and that was all.

It wasn't until years later that I found out that this girl went through a lot of pain after our breakup. That's one aspect of my past that I feel terrible about. I could have handled it better and brought less hurt into her life.

Even with the home pregnancy test, I decided to make sure by having Susan visit Dr. Gowan, my family doctor. I remember sitting in the parking lot after he had confirmed the news, holding on to Susan's hand, neither of us talking very much. It was early January of 1991.

We took a couple of days to make the decision that we were going to get married. Susan and I often went down to Foster Park, one of Union's prettiest places, to walk around together and talk about what we should do.

One of the things we settled right off was the abortion route. As soon as we discussed it, we realized that there wasn't much to talk about. Each of us was totally against the idea from the start. With all the other problems we had to figure out, it was a relief not to have to worry about making that decision.

We knew there were some reasons why we shouldn't get married. Susan had been planning on going away to college. Her plans were pretty fuzzy, and she didn't have a specific school in mind, but still, she knew she'd have to put that dream on hold if she were to have this baby, and she was disappointed.

There was also the problem of my take-home pay.

"Well, you don't make good money, David," she said. "You don't bring home but $170 a week." At the time, she was making low wages, too, working part-time at Winn-Dixie, and also as a weaver at Executive Knits, one of the textile mills in town.

"It's going to be tough, but we'll make it, Susan."

"Should we get married?"

"Maybe."

"Do you love me?"

"Yeah. Do you love me?"

"Yeah."

"We love each other, and marriage is the right thing to do," I said. "So why not do it?"

That was as much of a proposal as I ever gave her. The only reason we were getting married was that she was pregnant, and we knew that wasn't a good reason for marrying. But at the time, nobody could tell us differently. We said to ourselves that we would have our baby, and we would do whatever it took to make our marriage work.

We both knew what was immediately ahead of us—we had to tell her parents. Beyond that, neither one of us had much of an idea of what the future might hold.

When Susan and I went to the Russells to tell them the news, the four of us sat down together in the living room of their house.

"We've got something to talk to you about," I said. Not wanting to drag the scene out more than I had to, I got right down to it.

"Susan is pregnant," I said.

Beverly reacted to the news in a funny way. "Ugh," was all he said, just a single grunt, as if someone had given him a punch in the gut. He looked away, out the plate glass window, and he stayed turned away from the three of us for the rest of the discussion.

I almost burst out laughing from nervousness and from

the strangeness of it. This was the first time I had spent any real time with the Russells, and it was all kind of new to me.

Linda took the news in a more businesslike manner. "Well," she said. "Tell us what you all are going to do about it."

"We plan to get married," I said.

Susan was silent, staring down at the tabletop. *Help me out here,* I was trying to ESP her, but she didn't say anything.

Linda was frosty and remote with me, which I suppose was to be expected. I had screwed up royally in getting her daughter pregnant. At that point in time Linda hadn't met me more than once or twice for a few minutes, when I had gone over there to pick Susan up on dates.

There was no screaming and yelling, but I could tell I wasn't exactly Linda's dream for her daughter. She wanted somebody else for Susan, not me, but somebody with a college education, making $40,000 or $60,000 a year. That's what she thought that any daughter of Linda Russell's deserved—not an assistant manager at a grocery store.

But I couldn't worry about that. The most important thing for me was building a life for our new family.

CHAPTER

SIX

S omeone had sighted the Mazda.

   That was the news that buzzed through the Russell house early on Wednesday, the day after the boys had disappeared.

On the first morning after that awful, restless night, the whole mood of the house had changed. It had turned into a command post. The phone rang all the time. The members of the Russell family were there—Scotty, Susan's brother, had come over from his house just down the road with his wife, Wendy.

The Russells' feelings toward me did not change much just because we were in a family crisis. Linda's usual pose that morning and for many of the following days was standing in the kitchen or living room, smoking on her ever-present cigarette, looking tense and withdrawn.

Beverly was sitting in his big recliner in the living room. Moe, short for Michael—Susan's other brother—hung around near Beverly. Moe was thirty-five, but he still lived at home. I always liked Moe; he was nothing but a big kid at heart. His favorite thing was to get down on the floor of the living room, or down in the leaves in the yard, and play with all the family kids. Michael and Alex thought it was the biggest thrill in the world to climb over Moe's big belly like it was a mountain.

Susan's best friend, Donna Garner, and Donna's boyfriend, Mitchell, were out at the Russells', too, and Walt and Barbara, Donna's parents. The elder Garners were like second parents to Michael and Alex—they took care of them more times than I could count. Some of Susan's other friends, like Tracy Lovelace, came in and out that morning, and it seemed like the household was always in a state of confusion. There were some people there I didn't even know.

When Susan woke up that morning, she proceeded straight to Donna for a hug. Susan would do that a lot in the days to come. She would walk into the room—whatever room it was, the living room, or the sunporch off the den— and she would pick out a single person. She would focus in on them as though they alone could provide the comfort and words of encouragement she desperately needed.

Usually that person was me, but often Linda consoled Susan. If we weren't around, Susan had plenty of others in that house to go to.

Even that first day, before things got real crazy, I could tell Susan had the sense that she was on stage. People were always watching her. I thought she might be playing up the drama a little—but I had no idea how much.

It actually did turn out to be lucky we had the Russell house to go to. Despite the chilliness between my family and hers, they had a big place—big enough for the hordes of friends and relatives who eventually turned up. It was true what Susan had said that first night—our small Toney Road house would have gotten overrun.

Someone had reported a burgundy Mazda at a gas station in Sharon, South Carolina, about thirty miles up Highway 49 from Union, close to the North Carolina border.

That means he's heading north, I told myself. Toward Charlotte, toward a major city. A lot of people would see him, and he'd have to let Michael and Alex off somewhere. I thought this guy would drive through another county or two, park the car, and then be gone. Scotty and a couple of other people actually drove up to Sharon to check out the lead for themselves.

It was hard not to grab at straws. As the dawn brightened, more people started to come to the house. Many of them brought snacks or covered casserole dishes. The doughnuts that Susan and I had brought the night before from Winn-Dixie were just about snowed under by mounds and mounds of food.

Early in the day, my father called from California. He asked if I wanted him to come out. I told him I did. I was glad to get some additional support.

Tiffany called, too, and it was a big relief to talk to her. I knew I had feelings for her, but for the last twelve hours I had put them on the back burner, like everything else in my life, apart from my boys. I told her that I was holding up all right. Susan never knew anything about it. With all the friends and neighbors telephoning, Tiffany's call just blended in.

The only thing that was cheering me up, and what seemed to comfort Susan, too, was the vast outpouring of support we were receiving from the people of Union and the whole area upstate. The television was on when we went into the living room that morning, and it was really astonishing to watch the details of the search that was starting up.

Like a lot of other people, we watched the story of our boys' disappearance unfold on TV. Even at the beginning, we felt like prisoners in the house, afraid to miss something if we left. TV was how we had to get our information. The television was always on, tuned to news shows or sometimes CNN. It was an odd sensation, hearing the people you knew and loved most in the world referred to like strangers.

The sheer scale of the effort to find the boys was awesome. Of course, all the sheriff's deputies were involved, state troopers came over from Spartanburg, and SLED agents came up from Columbia. Because it was a kidnapping, the FBI got involved. Even Attorney General Janet Reno made finding Michael and Alex a top priority.

But what really moved me was how everyday people, not just law enforcement, got involved. To pick one example out of many, a man who owned a printshop in town, Mike Stevens, donated all the paper and printing costs to print up posters about Michael and Alex's disappearance. I had never met Mike Stevens in my life, but now my heart went out to him. There were hundreds of stories like that, strangers putting themselves out for my boys. Winn-Dixie also came through. The deli department donated fried chicken, biscuits and slaw for everyone down at the sheriff's office who helped in the search.

Union is right next door to Summit National Forest, and I remember one televised image I saw of people combing the woods, some of them on horseback, most on foot. I couldn't believe it. The best you can do in those woods is get infested by ticks, and the worst is, you might run up against a cottonmouth.

Yet here were ordinary citizens, people I didn't even know, sacrificing time and comfort to help look for Michael and Alex. The loneliness I'd started feeling the previous night was changed into an overwhelming feeling of thanksgiving.

"Come over here, Susan," I called to her, wanting to cheer her up, too. "Can you believe this? I just know they're going to find them." Susan stared at the tube without saying anything, then turned back to Donna.

That morning, they also showed police searching for tire tracks out at John D. Long Lake. It didn't really register on me. It seemed it was just another aspect of the search. The newspeople later said that the search there had come up with nothing.

From the description Susan had given Sheriff Wells the night before, police had come up with a crude sketch of the carjacker. They showed it on the news, and after I looked at it a while, I felt I just had to turn away—it was too painful. The guy didn't look evil or anything. Just like a normal guy.

The sketch was printed up by Mike Stevens on some fliers, and about ten o'clock that morning, a whole sheaf of them arrived at the Russell house. It seemed like everyone was relieved to have something to do. People shot out of that house with those fliers like a cavalry brigade. I remember watching a whole fleet of cars leaving down Heathwood Road in Mount Vernon Estates as if it were an auto rally.

There was a single news truck parked out there, too, that morning: Channel 7 had already arrived when we got back from the sheriff's that previous night. The next time I looked, later in the morning, there were three of them— Channel 7, Channel 4, and another one. It was like those news trucks were mushrooms sprouting from the ground after a hard rain.

Our relations with newspapers and television were divided. On the one hand, we wanted help from reporters in getting the word out for the boys, but on the other, they seemed almost like vultures, living off other people's misery.

"They want you to talk to the press," Scotty told us that morning. "You have to go down to the sheriff's office, and maybe you could do it there."

"Like a press conference?" Susan said.

"I guess," said Scotty.

"Sounds okay," I said.

But Susan wasn't so sure. She felt she couldn't handle talking to the media. It was just too much for her. She appeared overwhelmed with depression. I felt bad for her.

"Okay, honey, I'll do it," I said. "I want everybody out there looking for those boys."

Another thing the fliers had were great pictures of Michael and Alex. They were photos from a set that Susan had had a professional photographer take two months before, in a local photo studio called Sight and Sound. I had gone over to Toney Road that morning and helped get the kids dressed and ready, but I had some errands to run and didn't go over to the studio with them. By the time I got to the picture session, they'd already left.

The fliers asked everyone to report sightings of Michael: "A three-year-old boy, last seen clad in white jogging pants, blue-and-green shirt, a light blue coat, socks, and no shoes." And Alex: "His fourteen-month-old brother, who wore a red-and-white-striped jumper, blue-and-red coat, tennis shoes, and socks."

To everyone else, that was just a description of two missing kids. But to me, it was Mike-Mike and Fat Rat, my sons. I knew the outfits in those pictures. I had pulled the clothes on over their heads, had tried to make them stop squirming while I'd hiked them up on their legs. Somehow, those two bland descriptions, paired next to their photos, hit me in the heart. It really made me ache.

Susan loved to dress the boys up and show them off, and in those photos they were at their best. I will cherish the pictures always, because despite their formality, despite the fact they were taken by a stranger in a studio, they really bring out the incredible quality of life that was in Michael and Alex.

Michael looked like such a big boy, fooling around with and fussing with his "brudder." Fat Rat's light-up-your-life smile was in almost every frame.

Those photos were our secret weapon.

Everyone who saw them wanted to go right out and volunteer for the search effort, which is exactly what we needed to have happen. I wanted the whole country up in arms to find our beautiful boys. Eventually, incredibly, that happened, and the photos Susan took at Sight and Sound were a big reason for it. I think America fell in love with Michael and Alex because of those pictures.

Beverly came back to Mount Vernon Estates by mid-morning and told us the sheriff wanted us downtown again. I didn't mind that—anything I could do to further the investigation, I would. I thought it was stupid and asinine for them to be talking so much to us when they could be out looking for Michael and Alex, but if that's what they wanted, so be it.

To my relief, the sheriff's deputies got through with me fairly quickly that day, after the pounding I'd gotten the night before. They asked me again if I would agree to take a polygraph, and again I said yes, so they scheduled one for Saturday.

That session on Wednesday was when I told them that Susan was seeing other men. That got their interest going. Who'd she been seeing, they wanted to know, and for how long? Did I know names, details? I told them that as far as I knew, Susan had just broken it off with Tom Findlay.

But I also came right out and told them how I felt. "I don't know why you are talking so much to Susan and me," I said. For what felt like the millionth time, I told them, "Just find that car."

"We all want to get this thing straightened out," one of the deputies said, soothing me.

"Get what straightened out?"

"Inconsistencies."

It was the first time that I'd heard there were things that didn't add up in Susan's story. She'd told the sheriff that she'd left the house that night and gone to Wal-Mart to shop. Then she'd headed out to visit Mitch Sinclair, Donna's boyfriend.

Well, it turned out that nobody had seen her and the boys at Wal-Mart that night. Mitch hadn't even been home.

There was also the weird thing about the Monarch Mills stoplight. It had a traffic sensor, and the only way it was supposed to turn red was if there was a car coming the other way. But Susan had said that when she'd paused there at the light, there were no other vehicles there, there was no one at the light. It had been deserted when the car-jacker had jumped her. If that were true, there'd have been no red light.

I remember hearing all this stuff, but it was as if I had a filter on my ears. I never thought that any of it implicated Susan in the disappearance. Never.

She was upset. She was out of her mind. She said she stopped at Wal-Mart and made a mistake.

Mitch wasn't home? That was easy. We were such good friends that we dropped in on one another all the time. I knew Susan was upset about her fight with Tom Findlay. Mitch would be a friend she might talk to about it.

The stoplight? That was equally flimsy, to my mind. If you had a gun pointed at your rib cage, you could miss a car passing in front of you. Maybe the sensor had malfunc-tioned. The point was that questioning Susan was useless. She'd said she was not involved, and that was all I needed to know.

You have to understand that I was basing my belief in Susan on past experience. Whatever happened later, we'd had happiness and love in our family. Susan wasn't per-fect, but she was always a good, nurturing mother. She never lashed out at the children. Even after we separated, we did things together as a family. Susan was a loving mother. I never imagined she could be different.

"I just feel hopeless," Susan said softly to the reporters gathered before us. "I can't do enough. My children wanted me. They needed me. Now I can't help them. I just feel like such a failure."

She kept looking down during all this and would not face the flashbulbs and the television cameras. She had dressed neatly and pulled her hair back with a white bow— something that would be more or less her trademark for the next nine days.

There weren't many reporters there that first day, which was good, since it was our first experience with the press. Every time Susan paused, reporters would call out questions to her. Sheriff Wells had told us that we didn't have to answer any questions, just give our statements. Susan tried to explain the details of the carjacking.

"He made me get out of the car . . . I tried to get my children." She broke up, sobbing, and I was about to step in, but she recovered. She continued in a faltering voice. "I was saying, 'There's a baby,' and 'Please let me take them.' And he said, 'No.' And he just told me, he said, 'I don't have time, But I won't hurt them.' And he just took off."

I won't hurt them. I wonder if Susan knew how much that particular part of her lie meant to me in the days that followed. I clung to it like a drowning man. I had this faith, this innocent faith, that the man was telling the truth. *He said he wouldn't hurt them.* That line kept running through my head.

"I can't even describe what I'm going through," Susan continued to the reporters. "I mean, my heart is—it just aches so bad. I can't sleep. I can't eat. I can't do anything but think about them."

Then it was my turn. I tried to be as direct as possible, even though I was nervous as all get-out. I never did get used to talking to the cameras.

"I plead to the man. Me and my wife plead to him to please return our children to us safe and unharmed. We love our children very much, and we want them returned to us, safe and sound."

I went on to tell the story of Michael always insisting on having the door locks engaged whenever he went anywhere in the car. It just struck me as an agonizing detail, that a woman who was usually so careful this one time wasn't. And her little baby had been too sleepy to remind her.

CHAPTER

SEVEN

On Thursday, after a grueling morning of getting interviewed by *Inside Edition* and *A Current Affair,* I was happy finally to see a friendly face. My father had taken the red-eye from California and was waiting for me at the courthouse.

"Bear," he said to me, calling me by my boyhood nickname, already weeping. He had always been an emotional man. His second wife, Susan, was there with him, so now we had another pair of David and Susan Smiths. I gave them each a big hug.

I told them that the police had cleared me and I was no longer a suspect, and that they were now in the middle of giving Susan a lie detector test.

Susan's polygraph lasted all afternoon. While we waited in the courthouse, I tried to give my father some idea of what was going on. I had the feeling I wasn't being too coherent about it. I kept breaking down. My father has told me since that he knew instantly by looking in my eyes that I was in trouble. My heart was "under siege," as he put it.

Finally, in my father's presence, the floodgates opened. I just cried and cried.

My stepmom, Susan, hugged me. "That's all right," she said. "You don't have to talk."

I was so glad they'd come. It was good to have someone in my camp, backing me up. For the past two days, I had wanted someone to stay in the Toney Road house, just in case somehow, someone with important information—or even the carjacker—tried to call there. It was another example of my feeling so helpless that I wanted to do any little thing, take care of any little detail that might help.

I asked my father to stay at Toney Road while he was in Union, and he agreed. It couldn't have been easy for him, to move in among all his grandsons' toys, but I appreciated it immensely. Now I finally felt like we had all the bases covered.

Susan and I had now been apart for five or six whole hours. I told Eddie Harris, one of the SLED agents we were closest to, that I didn't want to wait any more.

"I have to see her," I told him.

"Hold on," said Eddie. "I'm going to take you to her right away."

"I'm not staying here a minute longer," I told him, fed up. "If you're going to keep me here, you're going to have to lock me up. Because I'm going now to find her."

"Well, then, let's go," he said. He took me into the little room they had her in for questioning.

The first thing I saw when I opened the door was Susan bawling, kind of draped half out of her chair and half on the floor. Sitting with her was an FBI agent, a big, tough guy with an attitude.

"David," she said to me. "I feel awful."

I was stunned at how Susan looked. Her face was splotchy and wet with tears, and she was shaking and practically on the floor. It enraged me how they were treating her. I understood that they needed to question her, but why did they have to badger her and make her feel so bad?

I put my arms around her and shushed her. She whispered into my shoulder, "David, they think I had something to do with it." Then she pulled her head back and looked into my eyes. "They don't believe my story!"

"Don't worry, Susan," I said. "You and I know the truth. No one else matters. They're just frustrated, too, because they can't find the boys." I sat with her and held her and waited for her to get herself back together.

"We're getting out of here," I said. I put my arm around Susan's shoulders and helped her stand up. Then Eddie Harris came in.

I said, "We're leaving."

"Wait a minute," said Eddie. Somebody at SLED wanted to ask us a few questions, he said.

"No, not another minute," I said. "We're leaving right now."

"Well, then, come on," said Eddie.

When I got her outside the room, Susan told me how badly she'd done on the lie detector test. "I don't know if I passed or not," she said. "It didn't go very good. They kept asking the same questions over and over. I can't believe how hard they were on me. I was like to break down in there."

I came out and told my father and stepmother we'd be

leaving in a few minutes, and that Susan had had a bad time with the polygraph.

Then Susan came over. She was pale and in tears and looked like a wrung-out dishcloth. When she saw my dad and stepmom, she walked up to them and allowed herself to be wrapped up in my dad's embrace.

"I'm glad you all came," she said. Then she said a word of comfort to reassure my father, who was obviously suffering during this emotional crisis.

"The boys will be okay," she said.

"Susan," I said, "I asked them if they wanted to stay over at Toney Road."

"That would be just fine," she said. "Make yourselves at home." She told my dad and stepmom to be sure to come over to the Russells', and we decided to meet up there later.

I was trying to get Susan to hold herself together emotionally, because I wanted us to do another press appearance late that afternoon. After our appearance in the newspaper and on television the previous day, the sheriff's office had received over a thousand tips. They came in from everywhere, from all over the country. The story had gone national.

Finally, I said to myself, here was something I could do that would actually help get back my boys. Every press conference, every reporter, every camera would help.

But Susan balked. "I can't face that again," she said to me. She started to cry.

"Shh," I soothed her. "It's for the boys. We've got to do it for Michael and Alex."

"I just can't do it," she said. "After what I've been through. You do it. Please?"

She nuzzled my cheek. I took her face in my hands and looked into her eyes. She looked totally worn out. There were large circles under her eyes from crying. She almost looked as if she had two shiners.

As soon as I got outside to face the cameras, I was glad I had let Susan out of it. I wasn't just facing five or six reporters now. There was a whole squad of them, pushing their microphones forward, shoving each other, shouting questions, acting like a group of people that had totally lost their minds.

I had to take a step backward, as if the crowd of reporters had physically pushed me. I was totally unprepared for the number of people out there. It was my first taste of what was to become, over the next few days, one of the biggest news stories of the whole year.

I summoned the image of Michael and Alex in my mind and stuttered out my statement.

"To whoever has my boys, we ask that you please don't hurt them, and bring them back. We love them and just want them back. I plead to the guy to return our children to us safe and unharmed. Everywhere I look, I see their toys and pictures. They are both wonderful children. I don't know how else to put it. I can't imagine life without them."

That night, as Susan and I drove out to the Russells', I felt tears burning in my eyes. Susan was next to me in the passenger seat, her eyes closed, resting. I was glad she wouldn't see me cry. I wanted to be strong for her.

Just the simple act of driving during that period was torture. I would scan the road constantly. And when I did see a small, dark-colored car, it would put a jolt through me that had me sitting straight up in my seat. I would stare at the car frantically, until I made sure it wasn't Susan's Mazda.

There wasn't much of a chance that the guy would be driving around Union, South Carolina, not with the whole country looking for him. But it was all I could think to do.

Susan and I were married on March 15, 1991. Right from the beginning, our marriage was overshadowed by death.

Less than two weeks before, on March 4, 1991, we had buried my older brother, Danny, in the graveyard of the same church in which Susan and I would later be married. When I stepped outside Bogansville United Methodist to walk off my pre-marriage nervousness, I'd found myself at his grave, still fresh, under a giant elm in the corner of the sloping cemetery.

Danny was only fourteen months older than me, and he and I had been close. Growing up, we did everything together. He and I would conspire to get out of our Jehovah's Witness obligations down at the Kingdom Hall. We would work together for our father and build forts together in the woods near our house.

There was about the same age difference between us as between Michael and Alex. If they had been allowed to grow up, I would have wanted them to have something like the close, comfortable, mildly competitive friendship that Danny and I had before he'd died.

He was my big brother, but from the age of eleven on, illness had cut him down to size—literally. Danny was suffering from Crohn's disease, a painful inflammation of the lower intestine, although for a long time no one knew that and he was tragically misdiagnosed. The disease gave him arthritis, hindered his digestion, and made his life a living hell off and on throughout his teens.

It also stunted his growth. I think in his mind he was always bigger than he was in real life. I was constantly pulling him out of fights that he got into with larger boys. Danny was a bit of a bully when he was younger. When he grew up small, he didn't change his mind-set. But Danny had another side to him, a joking, friendly, happy side. Everybody liked to have Danny around, especially at a party.

He died at Spartanburg Regional Medical Center of a sudden infection after what supposed to be a routine operation. We all knew he was very sick, but he wasn't supposed to die so young.

His death shocked me. I remember, in the days immediately afterward, I'd take out the all-terrain vehicle my brother had bought himself just before he'd died. I'd go back in the thirty-five acres of woods behind Moner's house, tearing around the trails, trying to outrace my pain.

My father took Danny's sudden death even harder than I did. He fell to pieces; he was lost in his grief. My parents' marriage, already shaky, collapsed under the strain of this huge new hole that had opened up in their lives.

All this was the background for my marriage to Susan Vaughan.

Susan's parents, Linda and Bev, didn't exactly help the situation. They very generously paid for our wedding. But beyond money, for emotional support, for welcoming me into the family or anything like that—well, it just wasn't going to happen.

Despite my brother's death, Linda had insisted that we go through with the wedding as scheduled. No delays for mourning. For Linda, appearances were everything. By that time, Susan had just started to show, but if you didn't know, you wouldn't think she looked pregnant. If we waited longer, though, there was that danger. Linda Sue wasn't going to have her daughter walk up the aisle with a full belly.

At the same time, Linda was coldly judgmental about the way the marriage had come about. She refused to pay for an all-white wedding gown. It could only be off-white for her fallen angel of a daughter, because Susan wasn't "pure" anymore. I wonder how she felt when Susan told her I never got around to giving her an engagement ring. I couldn't afford a fancy diamond.

With Danny's death so close behind us, March 15 was a doubly emotional day. My father was there with me at Bogansville Church, and he was having a hard time. He looked out the window to the gravesite.

"Well, make this a good wedding," he said, "because I'm only going to get to do it once."

Somehow, Susan and I made it up the aisle. I remember how beautiful she looked as a bride, how nervous we both were, fumbling with the rings and stammering out the answers to the questions put to us by the preacher. The church was full, and my father was best man, replacing Danny.

Afterward, Susan and I fed each other bites of cake and did the old routine with the garter. For that day, anyway,

Susan and I put our worries behind us and got swept up in feeling good about each other.

Linda's interference with our marriage didn't stop at the bride's choice of gown. Susan and I were planning to honeymoon in the Smoky Mountains, at the little resort town of Gatlinburg, Tennessee, a beautiful place. Everything was planned in advance. We had gotten a good price on a romantic chalet. We had packed our bags and stashed them at Moner's so we could leave directly after the reception in the church's fellowship hall.

We were at Moner's, changing our clothes for the trip, when Linda arrived and said she didn't think we should drive that far that night—it was a four-hour trip. She thought we weren't mature enough. I thought we should go for it.

After some hemming and hawing, Susan went along with her mama.

So it turned out we spent our wedding night in a Days Inn on the Interstate in Spartanburg, South Carolina. Not the most romantic of settings. I had the feeling that the ghost of Linda was in the room with us.

We had taken a step into our new world and gotten off on the wrong foot. I mentioned to Susan about the house out near Moner's, which I had partially remodeled for the high school girlfriend I'd planned to marry. By now, I had put thousands of dollars of my own money into renovating it, not to mention a lot of sweat. I knew it wasn't the Taj Mahal, but my grandmother owned it and would give it to us rent-free. I figured it would make a good home for us when we were just starting out.

Susan threw a wrench into those plans.

I took her out to look the place over when we were still making plans for our wedding. We had talked about it, and I knew she was worried about it being so small and having only a tin roof. We walked around inside, and I explained what I had done, all the changes I'd made.

"That's good," she said. We talked about a few things we could do to improve it.

Susan said, "I think we can make it work."

Then we brought Linda and Bev out to see the house. Linda didn't say much of anything about the interior I had worked so hard on. Bev made some suggestions. We could coat the aluminum roof to keep it from rusting out so much, he said. Out in the yard, Linda talked about putting in some shrubbery around the house so it would look better from the road.

After that, I would bring up the subject of the house once in a while. But Susan never mentioned it on her own. Her disinterest hurt my feelings a little. The house was just down the road from the place I'd grown up in, and it was about the same size. If my father could raise four children in a house like that, what was Susan turning up her nose at?

Looking at it through her eyes, though, I know what she saw. No matter how much work and love I put into our home, it would still be a tin-roofed country shack. Susan thought she saw the life she'd lead there: she would be out in the yard barefoot, a kid on her hip, picking collards for dinner. *Uh-uh,* Susan thought. *Not me.*

You've got to realize the gap between the way Susan grew up and the way I did. She was the city mouse and I was the country mouse. That made a big difference socially in Union, where city kids looked down on the hicks from the sticks.

Part of it was a class thing—there was a lot more poverty out in the countryside. People lived a real hand-to-mouth existence. When I was young, I was always the third boy in my family to wear a pair of pants. By the time I got them, the pockets had been worn out.

I was raised in the country, working in my great-grand-mother's vegetable gardens. When Susan was growing up, cooking some green beans meant going into the kitchen, opening up a can, and heating it up. For me, it meant going out into the field, picking the beans, stringing them, and putting them in a pot to cook.

I obviously didn't have the same prejudice Susan had. ''Poor but honest'' was the phrase from my upbringing, and there isn't any shame in that. But what Susan was re-jecting when she refused to move into my simple little house was my whole idea of living. She wanted something bigger, newer, grander. She wanted to move up from the comfort of her childhood, not go the other way.

Eventually, we compromised. Susan moved in with me at Moner's. My eighty-five-year-old great-grandmother, the one who had taken me in when I'd first left home, took my wife in, too. Her three-bedroom clapboard house had enough space for the three of us and the baby that would soon enough be here, as well. Moner was glad to have Susan move in, for us to keep her company.

Looking back on it now, it might not have been the best decision. Living with someone else, even somebody as generous as Moner, meant we didn't have the freedom as newlyweds that we'd have had in our own place. Take a

simple thing like walking around the house naked, for example—we couldn't do that. It made the uncertain time of
settling in together a little more tense.

Susan was also just next door to the crazed circus that
was my parents' disintegrating marriage. The fact of
Danny's death continued to drive my mom and dad apart,
and their fights were frequent and loud. It probably made
the disagreements that Susan and I had seem more severe.
Every time we fought, there was this idea that maybe we
were in danger of turning into my parents.

Things with my family came to a head one Sunday night
in May 1991. I'd worked a long day, from eight that morning. In the evening, I called Susan at home.

"Have you talked to Dad?" I asked her. He'd been saying off-the-wall things about suicide all week long, ever
since my mother had showed up one day to move all her
clothes out of the house.

"No," she said. "I haven't seen him."

"You might want to check on him." She called him several times, but he wouldn't answer the phone. So she called
me back.

"I can't get him on the phone, David."

"How about going over to check on him?" I said. "Call
me when you get over there. I'll stand by the phone."

Susan walked down from Moner's house to my parents'
place. All the lights were on in the house. She walked from
room to room and called me. "I don't see him."

"Where are you?"

"I'm in the living room," she said.

"Well, go back into his bedroom."

She walked over, carrying the phone. "He's not in

there,'' she said. Then she said, ''The back door's wide open.''

''Go out back and call him,'' I said. ''Maybe he's sitting out in the woods somewhere.''

But she didn't get an answer. Finally, I said, ''Go back in the house. Where have you looked?''

''Everywhere,'' she said.

''Go back into his bedroom,'' I told her, because I remembered suddenly that from the bedroom doorway you couldn't see the other side of the bed at all. ''Walk over there and look. Make sure he's not dying.'' I don't know what made me say that.

''Oh, my God,'' said Susan. ''There he is.''

My father was sprawled out on the floor, blood coming out of his mouth.

''I'm going to hang up and call the paramedics,'' I told Susan. ''You stay there and I'll call you back.'' I called to have the ambulance dispatched, but they weren't the first to reach the house. Two cops had already been on their way out there anyway, because a friend of our family's who worked the local crisis hotline had spoken with him earlier and had asked the police to check in on him. The ambulance got my dad to the emergency room just in time to save his life.

Later, my dad said he'd spent hours that day looking for his pistol, but he was so drunk he just couldn't remember where he'd stashed it. Or, he said, he would have used it. Afterward, he checked himself into a Spartanburg clinic to get the treatment he needed for his depression.

That incident turned out to be the end of my parents' marriage. They never got back together after that. My mother moved away from Union, to the South Carolina coast. My dad met his second wife, Susan, in the hospital, and got divorced from my mom.

Looking back, I can see how that event revealed something about our relationship, early in my marriage to Susan. She was strong for me then, when I was the one falling apart. At that time, I thought Susan was going to be my salvation from all this pain. I was still having a hard time with Danny's death. More nights than I can remember, Susan held me when I cried. She was there for me.

Moner and Susan had a good relationship, too, mostly because Susan was so caring toward her. I remember Susan bending down to help Moner on with her support hose in the morning in those first months we lived together. She helped Moner soak her tired feet in epsom salts at night. From Moner, Susan learned how to cook home-style food, so she could do her part in taking care of all of us.

In those early days, we were excited about both the marriage and becoming parents. We felt that despite the tragedies we'd both suffered, everything would work out for us. Susan loved being pregnant—she radiated it, showing off her belly, talking about how much she was going to enjoy being a mom. I was proud that I'd soon be a daddy, too. We spent a lot of good times fixing up Michael's room together.

Sometimes I would lie there and put my head on Susan's stomach, feeling the baby move. She would tell me when he was kicking, and I'd watch her belly to see the shape of his little foot. The feeling I got from that was indescribable.

We didn't know if we were having a son or a daughter. I would have been happy either way, of course, but I wanted a boy.

CHAPTER

EIGHT

T hursday had passed into Friday with no end in sight
to the nightmare of my boys being gone. There were
hundreds of leads pouring in to the sheriff's office,
but sooner or later, they all turned out to be false.

The previous evening, the disappearance of Michael and
Alex had been on all three national news programs. Reporters were trooping into town. Main Street downtown
was lined with satellite trucks.

They were camped outside the Russell house on Heathwood Road, too. Thursday night, they packed up and left,
and I thought we might get a break. But the trucks were all
back by seven the next morning. If nothing else, it showed
that the reporters were hard workers. By Friday afternoon,
there were cameras lined up all the way down the road, one
after another, waiting for something to happen.

We were like prisoners, trapped inside the house, behind
closed blinds. If I got a call on the cellular phone, I'd have
to tell whoever was on the other end to hold on a minute
and go to a different line. We had to use a secure phone

because we knew the media might have scanners to listen in.

If I wanted to go outside, I always used the back door. Even so, I could only go so far, because the cameras had an angle from the street. Some days I'd get so sick of being swarmed by the press that I'd put on a hat, pulled down low, and wear an old, beat-up jacket.

Every time Susan and I went in or out of the house, we had to push our way through all the reporters who wanted interviews. It was like an obstacle course. There was no peace for any of us.

The mood inside was starting to splinter up along family lines even more than it had before. One problem was that Beverly was used to being king in his own home, and now all these strangers had invaded it.

When my dad and stepmom came over from Toney Road Friday morning, they weren't welcomed so much as tolerated. Nobody ever said, "Hi." No one except me acknowledged my dad and stepmom's presence at all.

When she first arrived, Susan, my stepmom, came in and hugged Linda around the neck—a natural greeting, I felt, under the circumstances. But Linda backed quickly away, as if to say, "Don't touch me."

It was probably inevitable, given the history between my dad and the Russells, that they would get into some sort of dust-up. It didn't take long.

The fight was over Marc Klaas. Klaas was the father of the young girl who had been abducted and murdered in California, and since then he had been on a crusade concerning missing children. He had flown all the way from California to speak with us.

My dad lived in the same area where Polly Klaas had been abducted, so he knew about the case. He sat out near the driveway and had a long talk with Marc. He was convinced of Marc Klaas's sincerity and came in to plead his case to Susan and me.

"This man has lost his daughter," he told us. "He's got to have something to contribute here."

He pushed, insisting it was a good thing, but Susan didn't want to do it. "I don't want to talk to anybody," she said. "I'm worn out."

She finally left the room and told Bev that my dad was pressuring her.

When my dad first showed up in Union back in 1972, he really stood out. He was a freak, with hair all the way down to the middle of his back. He was trying to escape his life up in Detroit, which featured, as he put it, "too much wine and too many concerts." The Vietnam War had changed him, especially his second tour as an *Apocalypse Now*–style riverboat mortar man in the Mekong.

Almost as soon as he got to Union, my father had had an awkward run-in with Linda. He had found a job at a company where Linda worked in the personnel department. The plant manager interviewed him, liked him, and hired him. The next day my dad reported to Linda and said, "I've got a job here."

Linda Russell took one look at his long hair and said, "No, you don't." From that day on, he and Linda just didn't get along.

So there was my father, a guy who was on the edge of things, not in with the people who ran the county. Bev Russell was just the opposite, a good old boy from way back. It didn't take a genius to figure out what would happen if Dad challenged Bev's authority in his own house. Bev would pin his ears back.

That's what happened. Pretty soon after Susan had complained, word reached us that Bev and my father had almost come to blows. It would have been funny, if it hadn't been so awful—big, six-foot-five Bev picking a fight with my little five-four father. They faced off and Bev actually raised his fist to strike.

"You don't need to have that man out there and be talking to him," he now warned Dad about Klaas.

It was a bad, ugly scene, and everyone walked on eggshells around Bev after that. Marc Klaas left Union without ever talking to Susan or me.

The mood in the house wasn't helped by the fact that the flaws in Susan's story had by now been leaked to the press. Wells came out and told reporters that her account of that night had differed at various times. Of course, that only made the media wolves outside the door hungrier. They were howling for Susan.

I was frustrated by these new developments. *No, no, no,* I wanted to yell—*you're doing it all wrong. Go after the car, go after the boys. Don't go after Susan!*

The suspicions about Susan added a strange twist to the atmosphere at the Russells'. There we were, a whole group of us, watching a news program on TV, while a reporter asked people around the United States their opinions about the case.

These were ordinary folks on the street, and they didn't know us from Adam, but they said things like, "I just think the mother had something to do with it because this, this, and this just ain't right.''

It was uncomfortable for everyone at the house. Here was the accused, sitting right beside them. They all tried to show support—Scotty and Barb and Walt and Donna and everyone—but you could tell it cast a pall. It was as if someone had used a swear word in front of a preacher.

When the news programs started to focus in on Susan, I tried to shield her. I'd be sitting there beside her, too, holding her hand.

I'd say things back to the TV, like, "All right—you're stupid. Look for the car and don't worry about this woman here. She's going through enough.''

Susan said, "I can't believe they're pointing the finger at me. I can't believe they think I had something to do with it." Everyone would agree with her that it was sick.

I said, "Susan, don't pay them any attention. Those people are idiots out there."

When Tom Findlay called Susan right in the middle of all this, it was like a bolt from the blue. I didn't care at all that he phoned her. I had been calling Tiffany every day to let her know what was going on. Why shouldn't Susan talk to Tom?

But to Susan, Tom's call was a big deal. It was as if she thought I would turn terribly jealous all of a sudden or get my feelings hurt. She made a point to take the call in her parents' back bedroom. It was a big production, because she had to shoo some people out of there.

I was surprised when she came right back out. It seems they didn't talk but a few minutes. He'd just called to let her know he was thinking about her. Susan looked disappointed about how short the call was, but she was going to put the best face on it.

"I'm so glad he called," I heard her telling Donna. "Maybe he'll stop by a little later, if he can find the time."

But that was it. Tom Findlay never came over. He didn't phone her again, either. It was a one-time deal. Through some friends at Conso, the company where Susan had met Findlay, she sent word to him to come down to the Russells' and talk to her. But he never did.

Later, Susan asked if I had spoken with Tiffany lately.

"Susan," I said, "I talk to Tiffany every day. Okay?"

Susan got hot. "That's kind of unfair, don't you think? I've only talked to Tom once." We didn't have a fight, but she sure didn't like the arrangement, and she let me know it.

Still, Susan hung on to her dream. Many times during those awful, gut-wrenching days, Susan would put on a sweatshirt with an Auburn University logo. It was the one she had had on Tuesday night, at the McClouds'.

"Where did that come from?" I asked her.

"It's Tom's," she said. Tom had gone to college at Auburn. She wore it for our first newspaper photo Tuesday night.

It was as if she were trying to send Tom Findlay a message.

The first time I ever saw Tom Findlay, my wife was in his arms, and his hands were way lower than they should have been.

It was the Conso Products Christmas party in December 1993. Even though Susan and I had been living apart since the end of August, she'd invited me to come out to the Shrine Club for the party.

I was standing off to the side of the dance floor when Susan said to me, "There's someone I want you to meet."

"Okay," I said. "Who?"

"Him, over there." She pointed across the room, but I couldn't see who she was talking about.

"I'm going to go over and talk to him, if you don't mind."

"Sure," I said. "Go ahead."

But she didn't take me to shake his hand. Instead, a slow dance number came on, and she and I hit the floor together. Another slow tune followed, and we kept dancing. When a fast song started, we left the floor. I don't dance fast until I'm real intoxicated. I was getting to that point, but I wasn't there yet.

Susan said, "Do you mind if I dance with anyone else?"

"No, that's fine," I told her, and it was the truth. I never had been jealous of Susan in that way. When she danced with other guys or laughed with them, I didn't care. I wasn't threatened by other men if I knew there was nothing going on.

So she went across the floor and took Tom Findlay by the hand, and they started to dance.

I got a little steamed then, mostly at myself. It was obvious that she'd invited me to the party just so I could see this. Tom Findlay was staring into Susan's eyes with a loopy expression on his face. His hands were roaming around on her backside.

Like a fool, I had fallen right into Susan's trap. *Come out to the Conso party, David, so I can make you jealous.* During that time, our relationship was rocky. We weren't seeing each other all that often. Still, Susan was not above tormenting me with other men.

"Tom Findlay" was a name I'd heard around town once or twice, but I had never seen the guy before that night. I asked the people at my table who it was dancing with my wife, and they looked at me like I was an idiot for not knowing.

"That's the boss's son, Tommy," someone said.

You've got to realize what the Findlay family meant to Union to be able to gauge how that news fell on me. Back in the late eighties, J. Carey Findlay had picked Union up when it was nothing, when the unemployment in our county was among the highest in the whole nation. The mills had just about all shut down or moved out. Nobody was paying wages. It was like the Depression had hit the whole place once again.

That's what it was like in Union when my family moved there. But Carey Findlay bought one of the mills, fitted it to do fancy trimming work, and started Conso. That one mill practically kept the whole county afloat. It made tassels and fancy decorative trim. Some of the stuff was used in Buckingham Palace.

So around Union, South Carolina, J. Carey Findlay was a savior. He had a huge estate outside town—not just an upper-crust ranch home like Bev and Linda's, but a real mansion. Tom Findlay, thinning hair and all, was the rich bachelor of the town. He had as many girlfriends as he wanted. He had cocktail parties and hot-tub parties out at their big Findlay mansion.

Watching her dance with this guy was tearing me up. I

was pretty sure they didn't know each other well, but it definitely looked like they wanted to get to know each other better. As I stood there and tried not to stare, a lot of the Conso people were crowding me, wondering what I was doing. They didn't want me going up and bothering the boss's son.

"That's him, ain't it?" I said, as soon as Susan left the floor.

"Who?"

"That's who you're seeing."

"What are you talking about?" Susan said.

"I'm not taking this shit," I told her. "I'm leaving."

So I left. I stormed out and got a ride back to Toney Road. All was quiet there. The kids were over at Linda's, spending the night.

I had no intention of going back to the party, but finally I couldn't take it anymore. I called Tiffany to come pick me up in her car and drive me back to the Shrine Club.

When I walked into the hall, I couldn't believe my eyes. There they were, dancing again, all cuddled up. I walked out on the dance floor and tapped Susan on the shoulder.

"I want to talk to you," I said.

Tom said, "Fine." He wasn't going to make trouble. But Susan wasn't so agreeable. She was just about falling-down drunk, and she didn't want to go with me.

"Susan, come on, let's talk," I said. But I couldn't reason with her.

Then this big man out at the Conso plant appeared next to me and told me I was causing trouble. Three other big guys were with him. Everyone was drinking. By then, I was sober, so all the drunks looked wild and stupid to me.

They started pushing me, and I pushed back. People were shouting and tussling, and those folks had so much liquor in them that what should have been a small argument turned into an ugly incident. The four Conso men ended up shoving me out the door.

In the parking lot, it got even stranger. A woman Susan had worked with at Conso came over to me. She was intoxicated, too, and suddenly she was all over me. She actually lifted up her leg and wrapped it around my waist. I started staggering, trying to get her off me. Then, some other Conso women came over and started grabbing my crotch, laughing and whooping it up.

Susan had eventually followed me out the door, and when she saw what was going on, she got it all wrong. It didn't help that these crazy drunken women were saying that I was the one pawing them, instead of the other way around. I couldn't talk to Susan then. She was drunk and incoherent, yelling and cursing at me.

So I went back once more to our home. I thought Susan would join me there, but she ended up spending the night with a girlfriend from Conso. When she rolled in around ten the next morning, she was pretty hung over, but at least she was in her right mind. We sat on the edge of the bed and talked and apologized, and ended up making up with each other.

I couldn't help but feel after that night that a wedge had been driven between us. I told her later, on the telephone, what I thought of her precious rich boyfriend.

When Susan stood up for him, I knew for sure that there

was something going on between them. I didn't know what it was. I didn't have the details.

All I knew was, I couldn't handle it.

"Lord, we pray that You bring our little boys Michael and Alex back to us safe and sound. Shield them from hurt, oh Lord, and in Your wisdom see that the place for them is in their mama's loving arms."

Beverly had fallen heavily on his knees in the living room of the Russell home that night as soon as he'd gotten back home. He raised both of his hands and said loud and clear, in a voice you couldn't ignore, "Thank you, Jesus. Let us pray."

The living room of the Russells' home was huge. They had knocked down a wall between two original rooms to make one big one, and the final effect was almost like a hall. There might have been twenty-five or thirty people around the house that night—friends, relatives, hangers-on. About three-quarters of them did as Bev had asked and gathered around, taking each other's hands.

I got into the prayer circle, but my heart wasn't totally in it. For one thing, I saw that Bev had ignored the fact that my father and stepmom were still outside in the open garage. There were lawn chairs set up there, and quite a few people would congregate, shielded from the cameras of the press but still able to enjoy the fresh air.

Dad and my stepmom Susan stepped into the room while the prayer circle was still in its moment of silence. We all had our heads bowed. They stayed in the doorway, uncertain and uncomfortable. As I said, Bev and Linda did not go out of their way to make my family feel welcome.

And Bev's dramatic brand of testifying didn't much appeal to my dad and stepmom.

I wasn't going to quarrel with anyone who wanted to pray to bring back Michael and Alex. Bev had a good friend who was high up in a local church, and he would come over and pray with us a lot, saying long and extensive prayers. Other pastors would also drop by regularly and say a few prayers with us. They were having prayer vigils at almost every church in the county, where they would pray for hours nonstop.

But I put more stock in my own prayers than in the public kind that Bev liked so much. I would shut my eyes at night alone and try to will Jesus Christ to hear my prayers, to ask Him to protect my boys and lead them safely back home.

And I talked to my boys.

"Michael, I know you're taking good care of Fat Rat," I'd say. *"You know your Daddy loves you and he's coming for you really soon."*

I had such faith that it would happen. All the praying we were doing had to work. I totally believed that. If all that prayer didn't bring them home, nothing was going to.

CHAPTER

NINE

M ichael Daniel Smith was a well-loved baby when he came into our world at five-fifty in the afternoon on October 10, 1991.

Susan was overjoyed, and I was deliriously happy. Moner and my mother were proud. My Dad saw this new birth as a sun breaking through to his sad world; he was still affected by his loss of Danny. We gave Michael the middle name Daniel in memory of my big brother. Michael came from my middle name and from Susan's brother.

Susan wrote in Michael's baby album:

> I've been waiting a long time to see you, precious Michael. It was truly the most wonderful experience. When I heard Michael's first cry, I just started crying with him. I had given birth to the most beautiful baby boy in the world.

I was with Susan, coaching her and wiping her brow throughout the delivery, and the hospital let me stay the first night on a recliner in her room. We couldn't actually hold the baby much until later that night, because Michael's lungs were so filled with fluid that he had trouble breathing at first.

But when we did get him with us, he was such a little bundle of sweetness, a healthy eight-pound boy. I was over the moon!

I'd have to say that was the high-water mark of our marriage, that period around Michael's birth. It was a calm, hopeful time. We continued to live with Moner, who was by then nearly ninety years old, and it was a joy to watch the old lady with newborn Michael—her great-great-grandchild.

In those first months, I used to get up early with the baby when he first started to cry, heat up a bottle for him, then put him in his infant seat, so he and Moner could entertain each other in the kitchen while Susan and I went back to bed for a few extra hours of sleep.

Bogansville Church, where Danny was buried and Susan and I had been married, was just down the road from Moner's house. Susan and I took Michael and went to the eleven A.M. service as a family every Sunday. Sometimes before I went in, I'd sort of mentally stop and speak to Danny's spirit, where he lay in the Bogansville cemetery. *I'm finally happy, Bro—I'm a father, and my little son is a real star.*

After church we'd come back home to Moner's and have a country-style Sunday dinner, with fried chicken or cube steak with homemade gravy. Moner was old-fashioned, and when you sat down to eat, you got a seven-course meal and about a dozen side dishes—sliced tomatoes, cantaloupe, bread, green beans, corn—fresh from the garden, or stuff they had canned. Dad would usually come over to eat with us. He was doing a lot better by then, after his time in the hospital.

In the afternoon, we'd all just be a family together. We'd do stuff out in the yard, like wash both the cars. I was planting bulbs and shrubs, putting down pine bark, trying to make the place look more homey. If we were inside, we'd watch a football game on television, maybe, or just play with the baby.

My sister Becky lived fifteen minutes away with her husband Wallace and their newborn daughter, Kailly. She'd been born twenty-three hours after Michael. Kailly was a doll, and it was a lot of fun to get the two infants together.

Maybe if we had been left alone, and if we had more patience and understanding, Susan and I could have made a good life together. We were complementary in temperament—she was bubbly and I was steady—and we loved each other. We seemed to share a lot of values, like keeping a clean house and wanting to be decent parents.

We sure loved Michael. Whatever else happened later on, there was a lot of love in that house when our son was born. Michael never lacked for someone to cuddle and coo with him.

But even in that first year, with all the good times and all the good feelings, there were already tensions between us. One of our major differences had to do with money. Susan's head was always being turned by the things she didn't have. I remember that we would go over to someone's house to visit. Susan would walk into the room and see a stereo system, or a VCR, or a nice piece of furniture.

"Oh, I wish we could afford something like this," she'd

say. I tried not to pay it any mind. I knew we had money coming in, and we weren't starving. But I did feel it was a little dig against me, against my ability to support her in the style she'd grown up with.

Occasionally, Susan would go to her parents for "loans," or handouts. Bev gave us a new refrigerator. As an appliance store owner, he could get things at a discount. I was always exasperated when Susan asked for help. I wanted to live with her on my terms. I didn't go so far as to refuse the money or gifts the Russells gave us, but it rankled.

Part of the problem was my own stinginess. I hold the highest value to the dollar. That came from growing up poor, and also from my years of taking care of myself.

"Don't you even look to see what something costs before you decide to buy it?" I'd ask Susan. She'd look at me with a blank stare on her face.

Susan was a big worrier. She would get anxious about everything. What people thought about her. What she was going to wear to work the next day. But mainly she'd worry about bills coming in.

"There's a $200 phone bill," she'd say, "and we've got a $50 doctor bill. What are we gonna do?"

I'd say, "Don't worry about it. We'll pay them when we get the money."

"Where's the money gonna come from?"

"The money will come from somewhere, Susan. Just quit worrying about it."

"But Michael needs shoes," she'd say, "and there ain't but $20 in the checking account. What are we going to do?

He's got to have shoes. I'm gonna have to go borrow from Mama.''

I'd say, ''Don't do that.'' I tried to keep it light. ''His toes ain't sticking out the end of his shoes yet, so just give it some time.''

But if the price of something she wanted was too steep, she'd always say, ''Well, I guess I can borrow from Mama.'' Of course, that always irked the hell out of me. As it ended up, she didn't usually go to Linda for the money, anyway. I think she raised that idea just to get me going. She liked to do that.

That was mainly what Susan and I would fight about in that first year we were married—money and Linda. During that whole marriage, Susan could do no wrong, according to her mother. Everything was my fault.

I felt like Susan was still having her mother control her life. Linda would just show up all the time at the house. She wouldn't call first. When it came to questions about Michael, I'd say, ''Take this route,'' and Linda would always say, ''No, go this way.'' Susan almost always followed her Mama's advice.

Most of the time, we'd do what Linda said. Of course, it usually turned out okay—but that wasn't the point. I wanted to have the say-so over my own household. I didn't want my mother-in-law telling me how to take care of my children.

Susan talked to her mother on the phone constantly. She went down to the Russells' all the time. I felt like we had absolutely no privacy in our relationship. Susan spoke to her mother about everything in our marriage, even the most intimate details. We couldn't have our own problems—they had to be mine, Susan's, and Linda's.

Susan's brother, Scotty, told me that Linda had always been overprotective of Susan, ever since Susan's daddy had killed himself.

There were other issues between us, too. Moner was generous and loving, but staying with a third adult made it hard on us as newlyweds. We were frustrated by not having our own place, where we could hang curtains we'd chosen ourselves. It just wasn't the best situation, and Susan was especially impatient with it.

Being married and working at the same store also put a lot of stress on us. At home we were equals, but at Winn-Dixie, I was her boss. Once I was trying to stock, and I came around the corner and the checkout line was all backed up. I went back and found Susan in the office, socializing with another girl who worked there.

I said, "What the hell are you doing? Get out there. You've got people backed up. I thought I told you to watch the front while I'm stocking."

"You treat me like a dog," she said.

Susan could accept me telling her what to do—that wasn't the problem. It was the way I'd told her. I guess it was my fault. I should have respected that she was my wife and been a little more sympathetic to her. I take responsibility for that.

After Michael came along, Susan started taking birth control pills. The trouble was that she had a hard time remembering to take her pill every day. Sometimes she would miss two or three days. It would scare me. I didn't want her to get pregnant by accident again, but there wasn't much I could do about it. Every time we made love, we'd have to wait and worry until her period came. It was just another thing in our life together that made it so hard for us to get along.

That first year of our marriage, even our arguments were difficult. It was hard to have it out with each other at home with someone else around. We'd let things go, not talk about them, because we didn't want to fuss in front of Moner. Then, when we finally did fight, there'd be big blow-ups.

Susan would always threaten to go home to Linda's.

I did my part in all this. It takes two to tango—and Susan and I had some knock-down, drag-out fights.

Once, she confronted me about some other woman she had seen me talking to, and I denied there was anything going on. I was telling the truth, but it frustrated her. She got mad, words led to more words, and then she just got out of control. She jumped up and beat on my back, furious.

I only hit Susan one single time, when I lost my temper. I'm not proud of it, but it happened. She had been scream-ing at me that she would be better off if she'd never met me, and that she was going back home.

''I hate you!'' she yelled.

I slapped her in the face and she fell to the floor. Then I dragged her out to the front porch and dumped her there in a heap. I walked back in the house and slammed the door behind me as if I were through with her forever.

Later on, we made up. We always made up. Susan would spend a night or two at Linda's and then come back. I'd always apologize first.

''You're right,'' I'd say, ''I'm wrong.''

She'd respond quickly, and say, "No, it was my fault. I was the one who was wrong."

That was another way she got to me. We'd argue and argue and argue, until finally, I'd say, "Fine, you're right. I shouldn't have done that, I shouldn't have said that. I'm wrong."

"Well, no," she'd say, "it was all my fault."

That would make me climb the wall. But I'd just say to myself, *Okay, it's fine, it's over. Let it go. Let bygones be bygones.*

Pretty soon our fights were coming closer and closer together, so the times when we were getting along got shorter and shorter.

One time I was the one who slammed out of the house. I grabbed Michael and told Susan I would never let my kid be raised by such a witch of a mother.

"We're leaving," I yelled. "You aren't ever, ever going to see your son again!"

Susan was crying and screaming at me on the porch while I strapped Michael in his carseat and drove away. I stayed out ten minutes, and during that time Susan called Linda.

When I came back, Susan said, "I'm going to spend the night at Mama's."

"All right," I said, and I handed Michael over to her peacefully. The worst thing about fighting, for me, was that little Mike-Mike was seeing his parents act like idiots.

Maybe our fights wouldn't have been so hurtful if we'd stayed as close physically as we had once been. But something happened after Susan had Michael, and she didn't want to have intercourse any more. She had put on weight with her pregnancy and said she felt uncomfortable with herself.

I loved my wife's body and didn't care if she had gained a few pounds. I wanted to be close to her. I was a normal twenty-something male. I couldn't adjust to being shut down like that.

For me, my first year of marriage was like that Morton's Salt slogan: ''It never rains but it pours.'' On top of everything going on with Susan, I was still suffering over Danny's death, and I was worried about my dad. With all the bad things that had happened, and even the good ones, it was beginning to look like the most difficult year of my life.

Becoming parents. Becoming husband and wife. Setting up a household together. Danny's death, money, Linda, my father's attempted suicide, my parents' divorce, a new son . . . it was hard on me, and it was hard on Susan.

I wanted so much to make it work. I wanted Michael to have two parents and a secure family to grow up in. Looking back on it now, I think about how young and naive we were. It was a lot to handle, just starting out.

If we had gotten some help, if there'd been someone we respected who could have taken us aside and said, ''Look—it's natural for new parents to experience a rough patch in the bedroom,'' or, ''It's natural for new parents to have a lot of anxiety over money . . .''

Maybe that would have helped. But who could we talk to? My mother was gone, my father was a mess, Susan's folks were cold and distant, and Moner was out of a completely different world.

We were alone.

Finally, two days after our first wedding anniversary in March of 1992, Susan moved back home. Linda put a crib for Michael in Susan's girlhood bedroom, and our family was split apart for the first time.

I started calling Susan at the Russells' almost immediately.

It's true that I missed her, and I thought we could patch things up, but I also was lost without my son. I would ride Danny's four-wheel ATV around Moner's "back forty" for hours. For the first time in my life, I'd go out drinking with my friends, trying to get my marriage off my mind. But nothing worked. I felt terrible.

I tried to get us back together right away, but all my calls were met with a stubborn refusal by Susan even to consider moving back in. She would let me see Michael all I wanted. She was always good that way, not using him as a pawn. But I was getting nowhere in my campaign to win her back.

Then I switched strategies. I stopped calling her altogether.

That did the trick. After four or five days of the silent treatment, Susan started calling me. "Why don't you want to talk to me?" she'd ask. No man had ever treated her this way. She had always called the shots in her relationships.

So we started dating again. We were trying to work things out, put our marriage back together. Our relations were complicated by the fact that one of the men at Winn-Dixie Susan had been seeing just before we'd gotten together was back in her life.

Since he had left town, Winn-Dixie had moved and expanded. Susan's old boyfriend had been transferred back into the Union store when it had gone on a twenty-four-hour schedule. My job had changed since he'd left, too. I was a full assistant manager. I was now his boss.

Susan was also back at Winn-Dixie. She was supposed to come back full-time after her maternity leave, but the company had offered her only a part-time position.

Before the separation, it had sometimes been hard for Susan and me to be at work together. Now it was torture.

I saw her talking a lot with her old boyfriend, and it bothered me. Eventually, I realized they were sleeping together again. I wanted her to concentrate on getting us back together, so we could be proper parents to Michael. This affair she was having was a distraction.

"Keep away from him, Susan," I warned her. "It's not right."

Technically, their affair was adultery, even though Susan and I were separated then. Her lover was afraid of me and would walk away whenever I confronted him in the store. Still, he liked Susan, and he was going to enjoy this love affair while it lasted.

I caught him with her twice, and both times Susan had to pull me off him.

At first I had only speculated about what was going on between them. One night, soon after Susan had left me to move into her mother's house, she got off work at nine o'clock. I parked my Honda at Moner's got my grandmother's car, and followed Susan as she drove up to meet her lover in a church parking lot.

It made me furious. I parked on the highway about a quarter of a mile down the road and ran to the church. I'd never been there before, but it wasn't hard to see them sitting in his car. I ran over, jerked the door open and pulled him to the pavement, then began beating him with my fists.

He tried to get back into the car and got halfway in before I slammed his leg in the door. I grabbed him and slammed his head into the doorframe. I was out of control.

He was crying. He never even threw a lick back. Susan was the one who got physical. She jumped on my back, pulling my hair, trying to get me to stop.

"Don't hurt him!" she cried.

I backed off and said to Susan, "You've got to talk to me."

We walked off to the side of the parking lot, into the shadows. Her lover was still standing near the car, trying to get his bearings. I could see him bleeding as I talked to Susan.

"You are going to talk to me," I told her.

"I've got nothing to say. I'm going."

"I'll go kick his ass some more," I said. She knew I'd do it, too.

"Okay! Okay!" she said, "I'll talk."

I walked over and said to her boyfriend, "You just get the hell out of here."

He said, "I'm not leaving her."

I turned around and said to Susan, "You'd better tell him to get out of here."

"I can't tell him that."

"That's fine," I said. "I'm going to kick his ass."

"Okay, okay, okay," Susan said. "Go on," she told the guy. "Just leave."

Finally, he quit the scene.

Susan and I went over to the Russells' and had it out

some more in front of Bev and Linda. They told her she was wrong to meet her boyfriend at the church.

"Try to work things out with David," Beverly said. Linda said she thought we ought to work on our marriage.

The one time, Susan didn't blindly follow the advice of her parents was about this affair. I caught her with her boyfriend once again not long after.

This time, they were at his house. It was nine o'clock, and I was on my way in to work. Susan was supposed to have a class at USC-Union at eight-thirty. I rode by her boyfriend's, and sure enough, Susan's car was there.

I parked, got out, and put my hand on the hood of her car. I wanted to see how long she'd been there. If the metal was cold, I would probably have gone into another frenzy.

But the hood was warm. That was some relief. As I walked up to the front door, I didn't know what I was going to find inside. Would the two of them be in bed together?

I swung open the door and walked in. They were side by side on the couch, looking at some photographs.

The man went nuts. "Don't you ever, ever come in my house like that without knocking," he threatened.

I got him by the head then, and he jerked like a cockroach in a corner. I said, "Just shut up." And to Susan, "Let's go. We're leaving."

"I'm not going. Let's not go through this again, David," she told me.

Susan's lover was looking at me with fear and fury. "You can't make her leave," he said.

I kicked him in the shin, kicked him until he was in a fetal position on the couch, all curled up.

"Look at him, Susan. He's a wimp. He's a coward. What do you want him for?"

"That doesn't bother me," she said. "I know him. I'm not looking for that macho stuff. He's not a bully like you."

I didn't really have the size to be a bully. I just wanted to slam anybody who got between Susan and me.

Eventually, we left his house together and went off to talk things through some more. Everything had happened too fast. Susan was confused and so was I. But no matter how much we messed things up, I sensed that beneath it all we wanted to try to make our marriage work.

CHAPTER

TEN

The summer of 1992 was long and lonely for me. Susan was still living with Michael at Linda's. Even though he and I had spent a lot of time together—for his sake as well as mine—living without him left a constant ache in my heart.

Visiting Michael on my days off or on the occasional evening just wasn't the same as living with him, watching him grow up minute to minute. I'd always be thinking, "What if he falls down and scrapes his knee?" "How's he behaving himself at the nursery?" "Who's babysitting for him?" I had a thousand little questions about him that went unanswered because I didn't see him every day.

Just one example that I can give: it happened that Michael was born with his left foot turning in. If it wasn't corrected, it would influence the way he walked all his life.

Later, as he learned to walk, he had to wear special corrective shoes. But he was also supposed to sleep with a special bar between his feet at night. It was pretty miserable to hear him cry, banging that brace, the nights I'd be over visiting. But it was even worse when I wasn't there, thinking about Michael with that awful bar fastened to his legs, and nothing I could do about it.

The ache of missing Michael made me resolve to put our marriage back together in any way I could. My life without Susan and Michael was pretty empty. I wasn't seeing any other girls at that time, even though I knew Susan had her on-again, off-again relationship with her boyfriend at Winn-Dixie. I wasn't tempted to get to know other women. I was too torn up about losing my family.

All that summer of '92, Susan and I dated. It was a funny concept, dating your wife, but that's what it amounted to. We'd spend time at the Russells' as a family, or sometimes just Susan and I would go out to the local hamburger place while Linda looked after Michael.

Our sexual relations remained rocky, but we did occasionally spend the night together. I was as physically attracted to my wife as I had ever been. Susan was still self-conscious, though, about the changes her body had gone through after she'd had Michael.

Susan had stopped taking the pill after we separated this first time and we were back to using condoms, just like before we were married. We tried to be good about it, but there were times that we just didn't take the time to interrupt what we were doing to use one. That's how Susan became pregnant with Alex in November 1992.

Susan and I had a long talk in early December, when she discovered she had conceived again. For a time, it seemed that this was exactly the boost our marriage needed.

"You know," she said. "We've got to make this work. We have two kids involved in it now."

She had already broken it off with her current boyfriend.

There was never any question in my mind that Alex was my child. Some people mentioned that to me, later on, but I never doubted it.

We decided to try a fresh start. One important change we resolved to make was in our living arrangements. No more staying with Moner. If we were going to do this right, we'd have to get a home of our own.

Reluctantly, I agreed to follow Susan's suggestion that we ask her parents for a loan on a new house. I hesitated because I didn't want to be at all beholden to the Russells. But it was the only way we could afford to get a place of our own.

Bev and Linda came through for us with $6,000 that was half a gift and half a loan. That was the down payment that put us over the top.

It was exciting, going house-hunting with Susan. It made me feel that we had a real future together. We looked at everything we could afford, even trailers and mobile homes.

Finally, we found a small brick house on the northern edge of Union, just off the Duncan Bypass, a two-minute drive from Winn-Dixie. The Toney Road house seemed perfect for us. It was small when compared with Bev and Linda's, but it had three bedrooms, and Michael and the new baby could each have a room of his own. There was a generous sloping lawn out back and a carport in front protected by a fence.

This was just what we needed, we told ourselves. We were going to go all the way with it this time. We had privacy, space—a place all our own. We could knock a hole in the wall if we wanted to, knock down the wall itself if we felt like it. We had a good time planning for the future, choosing furniture and hanging wallpaper.

Even though we felt hopeful, there were some negative elements to our new life. The difference between how Susan felt during her second pregnancy and her first, for example, was like night and day.

When she was pregnant with Michael, she would gush to everyone about how happy she was. ''I'm just liking being pregnant so much,'' she'd say. Every new development was greeted with joy—the first time the baby kicked, the first sonogram. From watching her and hearing her comments, it was clear that Susan was a hundred percent happy about becoming a mom.

With the second pregnancy, she wasn't so cheerful. It was no secret that she was not so pleased with being pregnant a second time.

''Why'd I ever have another one?'' she'd moan. ''My feet hurt. I can't believe I have to go through this again.'' She was fearful about what another pregnancy would do to the shape of her body, which she felt was already destroyed. She said she was fat and ugly and was sorry she'd gotten pregnant in the first place. It was nonstop complaining the whole time.

''Look at my breasts!'' she demanded. ''They're so saggy.'' She had stretch marks from when she'd had Michael, on her abdomen, and on the sides of her breasts. She was convinced that no man could get excited over a body like that.

For my part, I never once ran her body down. It didn't matter to me in the least that she didn't look like a teenager any more. I was still attracted to Susan.

Springtime in South Carolina gets hot fast, and the spring of 1993 was no different. When you're carrying extra weight around, as Susan was with Alex, it makes things extra miserable. She vented her feelings a lot, making it clear to me that she never wanted to have children again. I know a lot of women say that during pregnancy and then go on to have more children later, but Susan was very decisive about it. I got the idea that she blamed me for her misery.

About this time, we stopped going to church together. It was just too difficult to get there. When we lived with Moner, Sunday service at Bogansville Methodist was a natural, regular part of our lives. After all, it was just a minute down the street. At Toney Road, something always came up to interfere with our churchgoing.

I was working long hours, thinking about my expanding family and putting food on the table. I worked the third shift all night long Saturday and needed to sleep in on Sunday. Susan was feeling so exhausted simply from being pregnant that there were times she didn't have the energy to do anything but sleep. And sometimes, we were just too lazy to drive to church. At the time, we didn't notice the loss of this part of our lives.

All during this time, Susan tended to shut me out emotionally. Sharing of all different kinds—talking about how each other's day went, trading anecdotes about Michael—seemed almost impossible for us. And sex was simply out of the question.

"We don't have to do it all the time," Susan said, when I tried to convince her to sleep with me. "Why can't we just lie in bed and cuddle?"

"Fine," I said. But how do you cuddle someone who has their back turned to you all the time? What are you going to cuddle, their shoulder?

"Please, Susan, please don't push me away," I remember begging, standing at the foot of the bed. I saw our love draining away and I didn't want it to end. She would just remain stony as ever. It got so bad that I couldn't even get near her.

Finally, something she said sent the message that our physical relationship was over.

"Having you touch me makes my skin crawl," she told me one night, after I begged her again not to drive me away. When your wife tells you that, you can pretty much consider yourself clued in that your marriage is in trouble.

I yearned to have someone to talk to, and I found her. That spring, I developed a friendship with a co-worker at Winn-Dixie, a friend of my younger sister's. I'd go over to her place and we'd talk for hours and watch television together. It was a heartfelt but totally nonphysical relationship. It went on for several months. We could tell each other our deepest feelings. For me, that included the pain I had over problems in my marriage.

I was attracted to this woman, but I held my behavior in check. With Susan pregnant, I couldn't have a relationship with someone else, no matter how lonely I was. But Susan heard gossip at the store and suspected that I was having an affair. Her jealousy represented one more burden on our life together.

At Toney Road, our fights were different than they'd been when we'd lived together at Moner's. It seemed like we could no longer raise up the passion to argue with one another. Instead, our disagreements took an even more hurtful form. We would brood and act sarcastic, or use the silent treatment. We didn't yell the way we used to do, but that was because we weren't really communicating at all. It was as if we had already given up.

We'd go to sleep mad a lot. Susan would do or say something that would get me angry, and instead of telling her how I felt, I'd give her the cold shoulder. I remember going outside and finding some chore to do in the garage until she went to bed, just so we wouldn't have to talk. Then I would come in and make my bed on the couch.

We were being childish. We weren't sitting down and reasoning like adults. What I should have done was take her hand and say, "Look, let's work this out."

Instead, I said the opposite: "Fine! I don't give a damn what you do."

Finally, though, at Susan's insistence, I ended my friendship with the girl at Winn-Dixie. Even though we were totally innocent, our knowing each other was not helping my relationship with my wife. For Michael's sake and for the sake of the new baby, I told her I couldn't remain friends with her.

I've always gotten along well with women in general. I can talk to them easily, and I enjoy their company. But I'm not a Don Juan, I'm not a womanizer. As far as going through one girl after another, that never happened at any period in my life.

My resolution to walk the straight-and-narrow crumbled when I met Tiffany Moss. It was only two weeks after I'd ended my friendship with my sister's friend. Tiffany came to work at Winn-Dixie as a cashier, and as soon as I saw her, I knew there would be something between us.

I was out of my mind with loneliness. Tiffany was friendly and warm where Susan was disapproving and cold.

I knew I was doing wrong. There's really no excuse for a husband to be dishonest and unfaithful at any time, but it is especially hurtful to step out on a woman who is pregnant. It's a vulnerable time. I took the trust Susan put in me and threw it away.

On the other hand, during that period Susan would always tell me she didn't care what I did. She put on a tough act.

"Maybe I should go out and find someone who cares about me a little bit," I'd say.

"Do what you want," she'd reply. "I don't care." She said it so often that I began to believe it.

The truth was a little different. The truth was that Susan didn't want me, but she didn't want anyone else to have me, either. Once Tiffany came along and Susan began to have suspicions about us, she tried everything she could to get us to break it off. That didn't mean she was warming up to me or treating me any better, it just meant she was jealous.

Susan and Tiffany had known each other briefly in high school. They were both in Junior Civitans, a club that does volunteer work. When Tiffany was in ninth grade, Susan was a senior, just graduating. They never talked to each other much, but at the end of the year, Susan did something nice for Tiffany. She thought Tiffany might make a good club officer. So Susan went out of her way to talk to the club sponsor about it, and Tiffany got to be secretary-treasurer the next year.

On Tiffany's first day at Winn-Dixie, I was working as assistant manager and set her up with some training videos and left her in the upstairs lounge to watch them. I went up to check on her after an hour or so.

"You okay?" I asked. "You need anything?"

"I'm fine," she said, smiling. "I'm not watching these videos much, but I'm fine." We both laughed.

It was always that way with Tiffany—nice and easy.

In the beginning, of course, Susan had no suspicions about Tiffany. She would come in the store and chat.

I remember Susan came in once when she was pregnant with Alex. She no longer worked for Winn-Dixie, but she was there pretty often to shop or to see me. She set Michael down on the conveyor belt in front of Tiffany's register and the two of them played with him while they made small talk.

During the summer, Tiffany and I got to know each other a little better. She would be checking and I would come up and bag her groceries.

I kept talking with her, asking her if she had a boyfriend. Just friendly flirting in one sense, but in another, we both knew it was something more.

She would say, "Aren't you married? Get away from me." Again, just joking, but half-serious at the same time.

Finally, something had to give. I myself don't remember exactly what day it was, but if you asked Tiffany, she'd tell you it was June 28, 1993. I was driving past Winn-Dixie one evening, and I saw Tiffany pull out of the lot and head for home. I followed. I pulled up beside her to let her know who it was.

Then I fell way, way back. I was trying to feel her out. Was she going to pull over or was she going to keep going? She saw me in the rearview. She was thinking, "What is this guy doing?"

We played cat-and-mouse all the way through downtown Union. And then I thought, well, this is silly. So, near Foster Park, I got ahead and pulled over in front of her. She pulled over, too.

That was when it really started. That was our first kiss. We stood there and talked for about an hour.

For a long time, talk was all we actually did. We would meet when Tiffany got off work or when I did. We would drive out into the country and park on a dirt road.

And we'd talk.

Looking back, I can see that's what I was lonely for—just someone to talk to.

I told myself that was all it was going to be.

CHAPTER

ELEVEN

On Saturday, the first weekend after the boys were gone, all the churches in Union County agreed to hold prayer vigils for Michael and Alex.

Driving through town, we saw a blitz of yellow ribbons. When Susan and I went to the sheriff's office to be questioned, we'd pass hundreds of them. They were tied around trees and porches and were being worn on people's lapels. The people at Union Federal Bank had donated time to make up lapel pins with pictures of Michael and Alex— one of the studio shots from Sight and Sound—and there was a ribbon on that. At Toney Road, the neighbors tied a yellow ribbon around the front porch railing.

Seeing Union with all those ribbons everywhere reminded me of how I'd felt when I'd heard those SLED helicopters searching for Michael and Alex that first night. It was comforting, in a way, that so many people were concerned about my boys. But I was scared, too, that this thing was so serious it had the whole county reacting to it.

It didn't stop at Union, of course. I was slowly becoming aware that my sons had touched the hearts of millions of people, not just around the country, but around the world, too. There were reporters coming to Union from Canada, Germany, and England. The outpouring of emotion was incredible.

While I was grateful for the attention because it might help bring Michael and Alex back home, it got to be a little overwhelming sometimes—trying to care for Susan, trying to help the search for the boys in any way, facing hundreds of microphones and cameras every day. I was a simple country boy who had never been interviewed before in my life. Each day there were more demands on us.

That Saturday, I was hooked up to the polygraph, one sensor across my stomach, one across my heart, one on my right hand. The sensor on my arm was like a blood pressure cuff with a Velcro fastening.

The thing about a lie detector test is that it is no piece of cake, even if you are totally innocent of any wrongdoing. As soon as I came into the room, I had butterflies. I began to sweat and second-guess myself. I worried that I'd be so nervous I would throw the machine off—start giving wrong answers, have it read "lie" when I was telling the truth.

The questioner was a young SLED agent, a polygraph expert, a nice enough guy. I was sitting in an old rickety chair next to an old wooden schoolteacher's desk. The agent had an array of polygraph electronics facing him. I couldn't see the needles—in fact, he told me not to look in his direction at all.

What he'd do was go along asking easy, yes-or-no questions—Was my name David Michael Smith? Was I born in

Michigan? Then he worked into asking directly about the case.

"Do you know or do you have any idea of the whereabouts of your children?"

"No."

"Did you have anything to do with this disappearance of your children?"

"No."

You could only answer "yes" or "no"; you could not elaborate. I was scared. I knew I was innocent, and yet I was scared I was going to flunk it. Everyone who takes one is afraid of a lie detector test. I told myself to be calm and think about something nice, like a waterfall or a field of flowers. Then I would just go ahead and answer naturally.

"Do you know where your children are?"

"No."

I only had to take that single polygraph. They never told me if I passed or failed. My dad and my stepmom Susan asked a SLED agent about the results of my test.

"He did fine," said the SLED agent. "We knew he would."

When I got out of the polygraph session, I felt as if I had been put through another wringer. I told myself it was all for the best, that now they would quit looking at me and put all their effort into finding the car.

Susan and I were inseparable. If she was at one side of the room and I was over here, that was too far apart. We wanted to be right beside each other. She would break down and be on her knees, crying. Her mother would help her sometimes. But most of the time, she wanted me. If I wasn't right there, if I was in the kitchen or someplace, she would send somebody to get me.

At night, I would lie close to Susan in her narrow girlhood bed, stroking her hair. She would turn her face away from mine, but my body cupped around hers so that every possible square inch of our skin was touching.

I didn't feel sexual urgings toward the woman who lay in my arms—I was way too rattled for anything like that. But I was scared and vulnerable, I wanted to be close to Susan, and I knew she wanted to be close to me.

She dozed fitfully, sometimes sobbing in her sleep. In those moments of tenderness just before dawn, as the sky lightened up and the birds started to make noise outside the window, I held on to Susan as if she were my life raft.

We were so alone, the two of us.

I could always hear the dim sound of the other family members moving about the house, keeping the vigil, answering the phone when it rang. My tendency was always to leap out of bed and get it myself, hoping for good news, but I knew we needed to rest and that they would call me if anything developed in the case.

The world had shrunk down to Susan and me. No one else could feel what we were feeling. No one had known the boys as we had, no one else had shared their joys and sufferings the way we had.

Because of our bond, I felt that I might be able to break through and help Susan remember the details we needed to find the boys. Behind closed doors, I would gently question her about the night of carjacking.

"Can you think of anything else?" I asked. "Did he have any scars on his face?"

"I told everything I can remember."

Sometimes she'd go back and add little bits and pieces to her story. The first couple of times we talked, she didn't mention that the man was breathing hard when he'd jumped into the car. Or that he had on a flannel shirt. Those kinds of details.

The mood in the Russell house was getting to be very much us-against-them. "They" were the media, the newspapers, the tabloid television shows that were out in force. We were very aware that our every move was being watched and analyzed. When we wanted to spend time outside, we went to the garage, which faced away from the road, or used the screened-in porch.

It baffled me, how paranoid Beverly and Linda were about the press. Hey, I thought, we should use them. Give them what they want; they'll give us what we want.

When Margaret Gregory came on the scene, things tightened up even more. Margaret was the wife of Dennis Gregory, a cousin of Susan's, and she worked in the public information office of the sheriff's office of Richland County, which included the state capital, Columbia. She was the only member of either family who'd had any experience in dealing with the press, so Bev and Linda decided she was going to be the official family spokesperson.

All contact with the press had to go through Margaret. She really ruled the roost. When a member of the media called the Russell house, the call went up, "Get Margaret!" If anyone from the media started walking up the driveway, it was, "Quick, get Margaret." If someone dared to try to talk directly to a member of the family, she would be firm with them: "We have nothing to report. This is private property."

Margaret also drafted press releases on behalf of the family, and she was a great help to us that way. But Margaret Gregory could not help me when I had to face reporters alone, to plead for my sons' safe return or to answer questions.

I don't think anyone can be prepared for the onslaught of media that happens in a case which strikes at the heart of the country. On Saturday, I stepped outside the squat, fortress-like sheriff's office, next door to the Union courthouse, and I was almost overwhelmed.

A semicircle of reporters, cameramen, and sound people were there to greet me. There were so many in town now that the Salvation Army had taken to feeding them all. I saw dozens of video cameras aimed at me, big cameras, little cameras. Maybe forty or fifty microphones, some of them on booms that reached above the crowd and hovered over my head.

Every encounter I had with the media was very stressful, very confusing. I'd be answering one question—"Are there any new leads in the search for your boys?"—and there'd be five other questions shouted at me in the meantime. People would be squirming for position in front of the crowd, and that would be distracting. Always, the flashbulbs were zapping off in front of my face.

The problem was, by now a lot of those reporters were asking questions about Susan's involvement in the disappearance of Michael and Alex. When Sheriff Wells had mentioned, the day before, that there were discrepancies in Susan's account of the carjacking, it had opened the floodgates. Suddenly the reporters were turning ugly, challenging me.

"David, do you think your wife had anything to do with it?" That question was thrown at me in a hundred different versions. I refused to have anything to do with that line of inquiry.

"I wish you all would concentrate on finding the boys," I said.

As soon as I could that Saturday, I gave up and retreated back to the Russells'. That night, the story of the carjacking appeared on *America's Most Wanted.* I was too upset to watch.

CHAPTER

TWELVE

D uring the stretch of time leading up to Alex's birth, the situation with Susan, Tiffany, and me just got crazier. Susan was on a campaign to destroy our relationship—even though both Tiffany and I denied there was anything between us.

Susan began harassing Tiffany. She would call her at the store, or at home.

"You'd better stay away from my husband," Susan warned Tiffany.

The first couple of times Susan called, Tiffany denied the whole thing. "I don't know what you're talking about, Susan," Tiffany said.

"I know what you're doing."

"C'mon, Susan, nothing's going on," Tiffany said. "I wouldn't do that to you."

"You'd just better leave him alone, if you know what's good for you."

Eventually, though, Tiffany threw caution to the wind. "If you could give him what he wants, then he wouldn't come looking for me," she'd said.

Susan got more and more desperate. She called Tiffany's mother and accused her daughter of being a home-wrecker. She came into Winn-Dixie and would freeze Tiffany out or threaten her. Susan never once screamed or yelled or caused a scene with me, the way some people said she did, but she sure gave Tiffany a hard time.

Susan knew the routine well enough at Winn-Dixie to be able to compare schedules and see whether I was supposed to work at the same time as Tiffany. Then she always tried to get me to switch my schedule around so we wouldn't work together. If that didn't work, she made it a point to come in—to check on us, and to make her presence felt.

I think Susan's behavior would have been more understandable to me if she had shown me any affection or willingness to work on our relationship. It would be one thing if I was cheating on a loving and sympathetic wife. Susan was totally uninterested in me, totally apathetic about our life together—but she obsessed over what was going on between Tiffany and me.

Tiffany and I were always very cautious with our meetings. I guess you could use another term, too: we were sneaky. We'd take separate routes to where we'd be meeting. If we thought anyone was following us, we wouldn't stop, we'd keep on going. There was a time or two when she stood me up, and a time or two when I stood her up, because we believed we were being watched.

The most delicate thing was getting Tiffany together with Michael. That was dynamite. We had to go to another town—over to Clinton, maybe, or up to Spartanburg—to do that. Still, I felt like I had to do it, because I knew that

Susan and I would surely get divorced soon, and I wanted Tiffany to know Michael.

She knew I loved Michael so much, and he was a big part of my life. There was no way she could know me without knowing Michael. It was part of one big package. He was all I talked about.

It was a difficult situation because Michael was getting to where he could talk. He used to refer to Tiffany as "that girl" and it always made Tiffany and me laugh. But I didn't want him to go back to Susan and say, "Me and that girl played in the playground," or something like that.

I also didn't want to confuse the little guy. He didn't understand who Tiffany was. He didn't associate me with any other female except Susan.

The night that Alex was born, I was supposed to see Tiffany. As it got later and later and I didn't shown up, she finally figured out what had happened.

That whole situation—having a date to meet my girlfriend and winding up instead sitting in a hospital while my wife went into labor—is just an indication of how mixed up my life had become.

I would step back and look at my situation, mine and Tiffany's, and I'd think, "This is a madhouse." There were so many overheated emotions, denials, or telephone calls where the wrong person would answer and you'd have to hang up. Just total chaos.

In the middle of it all, though, this wonderful thing happened to me. Alex's birth was a joy. I was able to separate it out from all the difficulties between Susan and me to see

Alex for what he was: a pure, innocent child, caught in an unfortunate situation between his parents.

Alex arrived via emergency C-section. The medical people kept losing his heartbeat, and they didn't know if he was strangling on the umbilical cord or not. It turned out that the cord was getting in between the monitor and his heart, interfering with the sound. It wasn't serious, but they didn't know that at the time.

I was allowed to stay in the room while Susan had the surgery. She had a hard time with it, and I was holding her hand, talking to her, telling her to just keep calm.

I recall holding Alex that first night. He was rounder and more dimply than Michael had been. He looked more like a baby and less like a little old man. I stared into his plump little face and swore to him that the storms of life which were washing over me would never get to him.

We named him Alexander Tyler—not after anyone, just two names we picked out of thin air.

"I love you, little guy," I said, and Alex gurgled and scrunched up his eyes.

Michael was so excited to be a big brother that he was almost beside himself. "Alex!" he'd call out, his eyes lighting up whenever he said it. I was a little stunned by it all. We were now a family of four.

There was a brief period when Alex's birth seemed to put a glow over everything. Susan and I were busy with getting the baby home and getting her healed from her Caesarean. We called a momentary truce.

But it was too late. There was no real affection between us anymore. Three weeks after Alex's birth, I moved out of the Toney Road house and back into Moner's.

After Susan had recovered from the surgery and was ready to go back to work, she decided to look for a new job. She couldn't go back to Winn-Dixie, she decided—not with me there, not with Tiffany there.

She got herself hired in the bookkeeping department at Conso Products. I think that decision—Susan's decision not to take up her old life-style and come back to Winn-Dixie—started a chain of events that eventually eliminated the chance that she and I would ever get back together. We tried to make our marriage work on and off for the next year, but we were just going through the motions.

This was not just because Conso was where she'd met Tom Findlay and the other men she would have affairs with, but because her new job opened a whole other world for Susan. She saw the possibilities that a really prosperous life offered. It also separated us because we no longer shared the same work environment. She had a whole circle of other friends I didn't know. Her old life with me was starting to look less attractive to her.

After Susan started working at Conso, there were other changes in her behavior apart from her attitude toward me.

If there's one thing I can fault Susan for—and as I've said, in all other respects she was a good mom to Alex and Michael—it was that she had this tendency to leave the boys at other people's houses while she went about her business.

We couldn't afford babysitters much and checking the boys with other people gave her the freedom to go out to shop or exercise or socialize. All of which I could understand, but I felt she did it too much, and I didn't like it. I even had a name for this practice. I called it "doffing off."

"Susan, why do you have to doff the boys off on other people all the time?" I would ask her.

She was always doing it. We were lucky in that we had a kind, loving older couple—Donna's parents, Barb and Walt—to help care for our boys. They didn't have grandchildren yet themselves, but the love they gave Michael and Alex made me think they were naturals in the role.

Barb and Walt took care of the boys countless times, never asking for a penny, doing things like taking the boys up to Walt's father's farm, where Michael could play with chickens, ride a tractor, do the kind of country stuff that he always loved—especially feeding the pigs.

Walt's parents, Honey and Pa were old-timey people, and Pa liked to chew tobacco. Michael could do a hilarious imitation of Pa, spitting out his tobacco juice.

At day care the husband of the babysitter would take two or three of the kids at a time to see the farm animals they had there. Sometimes, he would take some of the kids when he went to buy a cow at an auction. During these outings, Michael would stay right where he was supposed to be. He was a well-behaved boy.

Sometimes Susan would ask Donna herself to take the boys, or sometimes Linda—or me, if I wasn't working—but usually it was Barb and Walt. So that became Susan's mode of operation. She would drop Michael and Alex off at Barb and Walt's for the evening, or the afternoon, or the afternoon and the evening, while she went and did her thing.

All through that fall of 1993, Susan would doff off Michael and Alex with increasing frequency. First it was two nights a week, then three, then sometimes four or five. I saw the effect on the boys myself. They were always dressed well and taken care of. But they would be more clingy, and they would ask after their mama all the time.

My life with Tiffany was still complicated, even though I'd left Susan. I told Tiffany that Susan and I were going to divorce, and that I wanted us to be together. I wasn't just saying it; I wanted to believe it myself.

But it was difficult, with me living out at Moner's, to have anything that resembled a normal relationship. Tiffany still lived with her family, and her parents didn't know anything yet about the two of us. She used to have to wait until Moner went to sleep and drive out at midnight or so to see me. Then we'd watch TV and eat junk food and laugh a little until she'd have to drive back home to her house, usually getting in after two or three in the morning.

One time Susan brought the boys in to Winn-Dixie to see me. Tiffany happened to be at work, stocking some candy in the front of the store. I took Alex into the back room to show him off to some people there. Michael was pushing around one of those baby-sized shopping carts the store provides to keep kids occupied.

Michael took off with his cart, got right in front of Tiffany, and said, "Where's my daddy?"

"He'll be back in a minute," Tiffany said, "He just went in back."

Just then Susan looked up and noticed where Michael was. She jerked like someone had bitten her and started hollering at him: "Michael, you get back here or I'm going to tear your tail up! Get back here *now!*"

She came over and grabbed Michael and walked off, never looking at Tiffany or saying anything to her. She said to Michael, ''Don't you *ever* do that again.''

The message was clear: Tiffany was the enemy.

Given my relations with Tiffany, I didn't think it right for me to object to Susan seeing other men. I even had myself convinced that I wouldn't mind it. It was not until that disastrous Conso Christmas party that I found out how much it affected me.

I knew my heart lay with Tiffany. Susan and I really didn't have any future together. But the fact that she was sleeping around at Conso was more than I could bear. I had heard rumors about Susan and Tom Findlay, and about other men there, too.

Jealousy was snapping back at me in the worst way. I wasn't a guy who couldn't stand to see his woman glance at another man. When we worked together at Winn-Dixie, Susan would talk to guys she'd dated in high school, and seeing that would never make me mad. People should be able to be friends without breathing down each other's neck. Whatever jealous streak I have, I'd managed to keep it under control.

But it didn't rest easy on me, seeing Susan in Tom Findlay's arms that night at Conso's Christmas party. It convinced me of something.

If Susan was going to cat around and have affairs, I would have to leave town. I knew that even if I were to divorce her and start a new life with Tiffany, I couldn't live in Union and handle seeing her with another man. It would just be too painful. Maybe she could stand seeing me with someone else ("I don't care what you do," she would say), but I could never take that.

Susan's new life at Conso confused me. It made me think she was slipping out of my grasp. Against all my better judgment, I started seeing Susan again.

It was the early spring of 1994. I told myself—and a lot of other people—that I was making an effort to patch up my marriage because of my boys. That was the truth, but things were more complicated than that. I was also jealous of Susan's new affairs, and I wanted to see if the old David magic was still working.

I didn't tell Tiffany about it. It was nuts. I was cheating on my girlfriend with my wife, and I was cheating on my wife with my girlfriend.

Eventually, I became sure beyond a doubt that she was sleeping with Tom Findlay. It was late afternoon in March or April, and I went to Toney Road to surprise Susan with a bouquet of flowers and a bottle of wine. I was going to barbecue some dinner, play with the boys, and try to have a nice evening.

If I had been thinking clearly, I'd have known that Susan and I were beyond anything as normal as that.

I heard Susan drive up, and I went into Michael's bedroom. I was going to surprise her with the flowers when she came in, but something kept stopping me. I heard her open the screen door to the kitchen and then saw her as she walked past Michael's bedroom door holding Alex, who had fallen asleep in the car, on her way to put him in his crib.

She had left Michael to climb down out of the car by himself, and he was banging at the kitchen door. "Mama, let me in.'' So she walked back there to get him, and then I heard her pick up the phone.

Damn, I thought, I'm going to be in here forever. I thought how I would get Mike-Mike into the joke, making him quiet down as soon as he saw me. I thought Susan might be calling her mother, probably to tell her that she'd gotten home all right.

''Hiya, Baby Doll,'' I heard her say, and the hair on the back of my neck stood up. Definitely not her mom.

''I'm not doing anything—how about you? We gonna see each other tonight?''

I had to figure out who she was talking to. I waited. ''I don't know when I'm getting off tomorrow,'' Susan said. ''Depends when your daddy lets me off.''

Then I knew. ''Your daddy'' was Carey Findlay, Susan's boss and Tom Findlay's father, the owner of Conso.

''Baby Doll'' was Tom Findlay.

It sickened me to hear her talking to him. Findlay evidently told her about a magazine he was reading. ''You're looking at *Playboy?* You must be real horny.''

I couldn't stand it any longer. Impulsively, I walked out of Michael's bedroom into Susan's room, where she was sitting on the bed, her blouse off, talking into the phone. She'd already started to change out of her work clothes. Michael was playing in the living room.

Susan was so surprised to see me that she barely could react when I took the phone out of her hand.

''This is David Smith,'' I said into the receiver. ''I want you to keep away from my wife.''

"My boys, Michael and Alex. I loved to call them by their nicknames: Mike-Mike and Fat Rat. Their smiles would light up my life."

"Susan, Michael and me in the hospital. We were so happy to be parents."

"Here am I holding Michael hours after he was born. It felt so good to hold him."

"Susan was always a wonderful mother. One of her favorite things was to lie in bed with Michael and just look at him."

"I called my great-grandmother 'Moner' ever since I can remember. She was nearly ninety years old when Michael was born and helped us out a lot with him."

"Before we were married, Susan had this "glamour shot" done for me as a Valentine's Day gift. She was always doing nice things like that for me."

"When I look at this picture, I remember how happy we were on our wedding day and still wonder how we allowed our marriage to fall apart the way it did. We had so many plans back then."

"We spent our honeymoon in Gatlinburg, Tennessee. We rented a small chalet and enjoyed the week all to ourselves. We cooked our own meals and spent a lot of time in the mountains."

"Keeping a nice home for the boys was one of the things Susan and I agreed on. When we got settled in the Toney Road house, Susan worked real hard to get things just right."

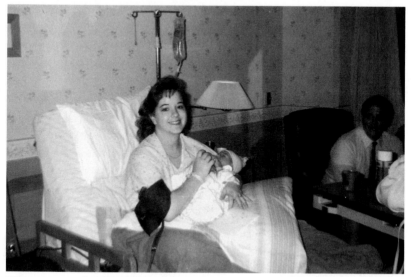

"It was scary when the doctor told us he'd have to deliver Alex by emergency C-section. The umbilical cord was getting in between the monitor and the heart, blocking the signal. But we all got through it together. Michael was so proud to have a baby brother.

"Six days after Alex was born, we were back in our home on Toney Road. Things between us weren't perfect, but we were together."

"Mike-Mike loved to help me do chores. He was a real daddy's boy and I enjoyed every minute of it."

"The boys and I loved bath time together. We just couldn't get enough of each other."

"Michael and me on Christmas Day, 1992. I never got to celebrate Christmas coming up because of being raised as a Jehovah's Witness, so we went all out with the boys."

"Michael got so excited about Halloween. Susan dressed him up as a pumpkin in 1992. We had the costumes all ready for Halloween, 1994. Alex was going to be a clown and Michael was going to be a pirate."

"One of my all-time favorite pictures of the boys. Michael and Alex loved each other so much. The little girl is Kailly, my niece, who was born just one day after Michael. They were inseparable."

"My Dad with the boys. He misses them so much."

"On the Thanksgiving after the boys died, I went with my Dad to visit family up in Michigan. He helped me so much with my grief and still does today. It was good taking a picture with him. We'd never done much of that growing up."

"My girlfriend Tiffany Moss came with me on the trip to Michigan. She knows me better than anyone and understands my deepest feelings about the loss of Michael and Alex. Tiffany was one of the last people to see the boys alive the night they died."

"Every time I see this memorial at John D. Lake, I'm overcome with thankfulness for the deep feeling people have for Michael and Alex. It doesn't always help my mood to visit the lake, but I do it anyway. And, when I do, I talk to the boys. I tell them I miss them and love them. It's hard."

"I've received over 21,000 letters, poems and notes of sympathy, along with thousands of homemade gifts, paintings and drawings like the ones in this photo. It is wonderful to me how much people need to show they care about me and my boys. I have no room to store them, but I can't bear to part with them."

"One of the few pictures I have of me and the boys together. I'd moved back with Moner after Susan and I split up but spent as much time as possible with them. Looking at this picture now, I remember taking that day for granted. I thought we'd have our whole lives to share with each other. I guess I didn't know then just how precious it was."

There was a long pause. "All right," Findlay said meekly, and he hung up.

All hell broke loose then, with Susan screaming at me never to come into her house again without asking her, and Michael and Alex starting to cry because their parents were arguing again.

But that stupid-jerk move of mine did the trick. Tom Findlay temporarily broke it off with Susan. In a sense, Susan was furious with me, but in another sense, I could see she was impressed. I put my foot down and told her enough was enough. Maybe that's what she'd been looking for all along.

About a week later, I moved back into Toney Road, and Susan and I were all set to give our marriage another chance.

When I told Tiffany I was going back to Susan, it really rocked her world. She felt totally betrayed.

Here I had been telling her all this time that we would get a place together, that Susan and I would divorce, and that she and I would finally be together without having to slip around. Suddenly, out of the blue, there I was, back at Toney Road.

Tiffany went a little crazy. I tried to tell her that the reason I was trying it again with Susan was because of the boys, but she just didn't buy it.

"You told me you were leaving her for good," she said. "And now you're going back." She didn't want to lose me. She told me she was willing to do anything to keep us together.

Tiffany started acting strange. Susan and I would be

home with the boys, and suddenly I'd hear Tiffany outside in the street, driving past the house and blowing her horn.

Tiffany said it was supposed to be some sort of signal. I thought it was stupid.

She did it night after night. Afterward, she would go back to Winn-Dixie and park. Sometimes she'd stay there three or four hours, waiting for me to meet her. Then she would drive back to the house and cruise past it again, leaning on that horn. Susan knew who it was, of course.

All the arguments we had now were about Tiffany: "That damned bitch keeps riding by," Susan said.

I played dumb. "I don't know if it's her or not."

"You're still talking to her," Susan said. "You're still seeing her!" I denied it.

When Tiffany called on the phone, if Susan answered, she'd hang up. If I picked up the phone and Susan happened to be in the room, I'd act like it was one of my buddies calling.

"Hey, yeah, boy, I'll get the rifle to you. Phone me. I gotta go."

Of course, that would only enrage Tiffany. The harassment intensified. She would ride by at three A.M.

Beep, beep, beep.

The neighbors were starting to complain.

"You've got to stop," I pleaded with Tiffany at work. "This is just wrong. You've got to quit riding by my house."

Between the two of them, it was more than I could bear. I felt like I was being torn apart.

During that brief last time I lived with Susan, it was

clear to both of us that we couldn't stay together—because of Tiffany, and for a lot of other reasons, too.

On my birthday, July 27, 1994, we took the boys out to Moner's for a birthday dinner. When we left, Susan took Alex, and I followed her to Toney Road with Michael. After we gave the boys their baths and put them to sleep, we sat on the living room couch together. It was like a quiet period in the midst of a storm.

Suddenly Susan just blurted it out: "I think I want a divorce."

Even though part of me knew it was inevitable, when it happened, I was filled with panic and remorse.

"Why?"

She looked at me, tears brimming in her eyes. "I'm so unhappy."

I cried with her, too. I thought about the road we had traveled together, the boys who were sleeping soundly in their bedrooms. I felt awful, like I had failed them most of all.

CHAPTER

THIRTEEN

Time after time during those endless nine days when the boys were lost, my hopes were raised by each new lead, only to have them dashed just as quickly when the leads didn't pan out.

On Wednesday, a trucker in Anderson County, near the Georgia border, radioed in to police that he'd seen an abandoned compact car that resembled Susan's parked next to the side of the road. Authorities immediately went to the scene, but no car was ever found.

Also on Wednesday, a Mazda that resembled Susan's was spotted on S.C. 321 in Chester County. No further sightings were reported.

On Thursday, a man who robbed a Salisbury, North Carolina, convenience store supposedly resembled the sketch that Susan had made of the carjacker. He was not the man.

On Friday, a child was heard crying in Uwharrie National Forest, northeast of Charlotte, North Carolina. An organized search by authorities on horseback and on foot turned up nothing.

Also on Friday, someone reported seeing a black man

covered with mud coming out of a wooded area near the Buena Vista Apartments in Union. Practically the whole press corps followed some sheriff's deputies over there. While a SLED helicopter hovered overhead, police dogs were brought in to search the area. The reporters waited all day out in the road for something to happen. Nothing ever did.

Finally, saddest of all, deputies who were searching the area around John D. Long Lake discovered some articles of children's clothing. They were soon discounted as not belonging to Michael and Alex.

Susan's description of the carjacker as black was stirring up race relations in Union. It was a southern town, after all, and not that far removed from the times when things had been segregated.

To me, it wasn't a racial issue. I only accused a black man because I believed Susan. I was sorry to see the trouble her description had caused. There were black people who were extremely nice to me all during those nine days. They brought food to the Russells' and gave me their sympathy.

But they were hauling in black men from all over Union County, and from what I heard, interrogating the hell out of them. One deputy told me that if they ever caught the guy, he wouldn't make it to the jail.

"We'd see that justice was served," he told me grimly.

I could understand that the black community was upset. It was just another aspect of the whole horrible situation.

By Sunday in the Russell home, we were all wrung out from being on such an emotional roller-coaster all week long. It was agonizing.

Through all of it, I only had Susan. I felt that we were together in our own world of grief and anguish.

As the days went by and Tom Findlay didn't call, didn't visit, didn't fulfill the fantasy that Susan obviously had of him, Susan turned to me. She was more tender than she'd been in years.

On Sunday evening we lay in bed together, talking about the boys. ''I promise you,'' she told me solemnly, ''when all this is over, we'll be together.''

I made a promise back to her. ''When the boys get back,'' I said, we would be a family again.

She hesitated. ''Even if they don't come back, you and me can still make it work,'' she said.

''Susan, Susan—we'll get Michael and Alex home,'' I said. ''Don't worry about anything else now.''

It might be hard to believe, but even then, five nights, 120 hours after the boys were taken, I still maintained a bed-rock sense of optimism. They *were* going to come back home. I believed it as much as I believed that the sun was going to come up the next morning.

But the nights were long. Susan was turning increasingly negative, and so I had the additional duty of keeping her spirits up.

''David, they aren't ever going to find those kids!'' Sort of moaning it out. She would actually sink to the floor, sobbing.

I'd take her face in my hands and stare into her eyes. ''They'll find them, Susan. Michael and Alex are safe. They'll be in your arms soon.'' At that time, I thought her negativity was coming from the intense interrogations she was being put through by the investigators.

I complained to Sheriff Wells about how hard they were treating Susan. For her next round of talks, her lead interrogator was a fatherly, older SLED agent who treated her much less harshly than the FBI had. It wasn't good cop, bad cop—they just changed their whole approach.

Sometimes it wasn't just the police I had to try to shield Susan from. The sheriff transferred Susan's questioning and polygraphs to the National Guard Armory on the west side of Union, away from Main Street, because the media pressure near the courthouse and sheriff's office was just too great.

From Monday on, that was where I took Susan every morning. I waited for her all day and took her home every night.

Beverly and Linda waited there, too, in a different room, all the way on the other side of the Armory, as if to emphasize the gulf between us. My dad and stepmom would come keep me company most of the time.

But even before Susan started her polygraph on Monday morning, I had to intercede in a scene between daughter and mother.

We had all gathered around Susan, telling her not to worry about her interview.

Suddenly Linda grabbed her daughter by the shoulders. "Susan, just tell them what you know!" Linda shouted at her, shaking her roughly. "If you are not telling the truth, you'd better tell the truth!"

"Mama, I am telling the truth!" Susan wailed.

After seeing the state the FBI agent had put Susan in a

few days earlier, I wasn't going to let anyone be rough on her. I found myself actually putting my arm in between them and pushing Linda away. She gave me a surprised look, as if I had slapped her face.

I didn't care. If the whole world had been against Susan then—and sometimes in those nine days it seemed as if it was—I would be the one holdout. I would be there for her.

At Linda's house later on, I took Susan aside and tried to help her. She was crying out of frustration. She had had a lie detector test on Thursday, Saturday, and that Monday, and she was scheduled for another one the next day.

"Those lie detector tests are rattling your nerves," I said. "You've just got to calm down to take them."

"I get so upset," she said.

"I know you do. I got upset, too. You want to know what I did?"

"What?" she asked.

"Whenever I came to one of those hard questions, those stumpers, you know—about the boys and all—and I was afraid I was just going to be too nervous to answer it, I'd close my eyes."

She looked at me. "Just close my eyes?"

"Close your eyes," I said. "Think of something peaceful. Think of a waterfall, or a field full of daisies with sunlight on them."

It was a very nervous Halloween in Union that year. Parents kept their kids off the street. Towns went out of their way to schedule indoor activities, like the traveling circus that put on its show in Buffalo.

We only watched the local and national news while we

were at Linda's. No one was interested in that tabloid trash. But I was learning the ways of tabloid television, how twisted they could make the truth, how they could slant things and exaggerate them until you couldn't recognize events that you yourself had lived through. Of all the media attracted to Union on the story, the people who worked for *A Current Affair* and *Inside Edition* were the worst.

On Monday evening, the TV program *A Current Affair* featured an interview with Mitch Sinclair, Donna Garner's boyfriend. Susan had said she'd been on the way over to visit Mitch when she'd been carjacked.

The show that featured Mitch was an example of how bad some shows could be. He was one of my best friends, a person I spent a lot of time with. He was usually present at the Russell house during those nine days, and he helped out with many of the search teams.

Yet from what people said, the show came off making him seem a little sinister. It reported that he didn't pass a polygraph test. A person who didn't know Mitch could conclude that he'd had something to do with the carjacking. The program even seemed to hint that Susan and he were having an affair.

Susan's reaction to this last bit was immediate. ''I would never sleep with somebody like Mitch!'' she said, laughing at the very idea. ''How could anyone think that?''

But Mitch's appearance on the show was enough to fan the flames of suspicion against Susan. ''The truth will come out,'' he said, as if he knew some deep, dark secret. Mitch told us that it was just a case of him being nervous and not knowing what to say.

On television, though, it came across sounding bad. The

next day, Tuesday, Sheriff Wells called Mitch in for questioning, grilling him about what he'd said on the show. Of course, he was quickly cleared of suspicion. All of which meant, to me, that the investigation wasn't going that well. When you get your leads off tabloid television, you're not making headway.

Even so, I still kept hold of my optimism. Susan was sleeping a lot—more than anyone else, it turned out. Bev and Linda would be up late, Dad and my stepmom would hardly lie down, I would be pacing the floor, but Susan would be sleeping soundly in the back bedroom. She'd sleep during the daytime, too, despite all the noise and activity in the house. She'd take her sedatives and just go off to nap by herself.

Occasionally, I would go in and stay with her while she slept, holding her, trying to watch over her. I remember being in the room on Monday and thinking about Halloween in the past. The previous year, Michael had gone out as a Keebler elf. It was a cute costume, and one Susan had gone out of her way to find.

This would have been the boys' first real Halloween going out trick-or-treating together. Since my family could never celebrate any holidays because of my mother's Jehovah's Witness beliefs, I wanted to make up for lost time. So we did holidays big-time. This year, Michael and Alex already had their Halloween costumes set: Mike-Mike was going as a pirate, and Fat Rat was going to be a clown.

We didn't stop at Halloween, either. Christmas, Easter, Fourth of July, Thanksgiving—I think we would have celebrated Lincoln's birthday if we could have found a stovepipe hat for Michael to wear. If I ever gave Susan an anniversary present or a birthday present, I would always get Michael something so he'd have one to open up, too, so he wouldn't feel left out.

Like every other kid, Michael enjoyed Christmas morning, especially as he was getting older. Susan always did some pretty good decorating around the house, and we always had a nice-looking Christmas tree and lots of gifts. The biggest gift Michael got his last Christmas was a plastic workbench.

Memories. Good and bad. Sitting in the bedroom that night, watching Susan sleep, they were all I had.

Michael's third birthday party was at the local McDonald's. I was working so I couldn't go. On the day of his birthday, though, I took him a little present, a plastic race car, the kind kids like to bang up and knock around. He was so happy when he unwrapped it. Ripping apart the wrapping paper on a present was always the fun part for Michael. I got down among the wrapping paper with him and we rolled around, laughing and giggling. That race car just had to wait to get played with for a little while.

If I had to pick a single memory out to remember Michael and Alex by, it wouldn't be any special day, like a birthday or holiday. I cherish the everyday times the most. The odd thing about them is that while you're living them, they seem to pass by without you even noticing them. But afterwards, looking back, those moments wind up being the ones that are most important.

I didn't have a private backyard at my apartment, so what the boys and I did was make Foster Park into our own playground. Almost every Sunday they spent with me I wound up taking them down there. It had some of the tallest trees in the county, and it was always shady and cool. The pond there had a flock of ducks that stayed there year-round.

The last time we went to the park to feed the ducks, Michael stood back, keeping a close eye on them. I could see he was torn two ways. He was afraid of the ducks, but he liked to feed them. I had to smile at him, but at the same time I wanted him to be courageous.

I was holding Alex in my arms. We had brought old bread that I'd saved up. Alex would break off a piece and throw it to them, and then the mallards would start quacking, wanting more.

The ducks rushed us a little, and they started crowding around Michael. He got all tore up and nervous, and he came over to me and hugged my leg.

"Hold me! Hold me!" he said. He was excited and scared at the same time, and wanted me to pick him up. I got him up in the crook of one arm, and I was holding Alex in the other. The boys laughed like crazy when I kind of chased the ducks back away from us so I could put Michael down again.

We finally got tired of the ducks that day and Michael dragged us over to the playground equipment. As Alex got bigger, the two of them could play on the slides for hours. Michael stood up on the big slide. I lifted Alex up and put him up at the very top of the slide, next to his brother.

"Okay, Alex?" Michael said. "You ready to go, Alex?" Alex was only fourteen months, so he wasn't talking yet, but Michael always asked if he was ready anyway. Michael gave him a shove and Alex slid down, laughing. I grabbed him and put him back up on top and the two of them went through it all again. Sometimes Michael would hold Alex in his lap and they'd slide down together. Alex would just beam out his smile all the way coming down with his big brother.

It was amazing what Michael and Alex could do, even as young as they were. Little athletes, both of them. There was a play fortress at Foster Park. It didn't have a top, just the outline, and a little ladder on the inside up to a pole you could slide down. Alex couldn't slide yet, but he could climb the ladder all the way to the top. I lifted Michael onto the pole and helped him slide down it, fireman style. I was proud of my boys for being so daring, but worried they might fall down and hurt themselves, so I stood close underneath just in case.

FOURTEEN

The only person I was keeping in touch with, outside the tight circle of the Russell household, was Tiffany. After the first few days, since Margaret Gregory took over handling the outside calls, Tiffany could no longer call the house directly and ask for me. She was still seen as the ''other woman'' by Linda and Bev, and no one was going to do her any favors.

But I would call her anyway. Speaking to Tiffany made me feel confused, since I still had strong feelings for her. Yet at the same time, Susan and I were whispering at night that we were going to reconcile, drop the divorce, and spend the rest of our lives as husband and wife.

Tiffany's life was being turned upside down, just as ours was. She didn't eat, didn't sleep. She'd sit up and wait until the three o'clock news came on, go to sleep for three hours, and when the six o'clock news came on in the morning, she was up again. Had the boys been found? Was there any sign of them? Unlike my other friends, Tiffany couldn't come to the Russell house and sit and wait with everybody for something to break. She had to get her information from the TV news.

She needed me, and she felt that she should be there for me, but we couldn't be together. I told her I had to be with Susan now, because that was the way we'd get the kids back.

"Okay, I understand that," she said. She said to me over and over when we would talk on the phone and she would try to lift my spirits: "Get those kids back—I'm ready to see them." Or, "Today, I just feel sure they're gonna find them."

After Susan asked for the divorce that summer, I was with Tiffany for real.

Susan even encouraged us. She dropped her coldness toward Tiffany and sympathized with her. "You know that me and David are not going to work things out," she told Tiffany on the phone. "We just can't get along. You and him would be good together. I think you would take care of Michael and Alex. I want him to see you."

Tiffany didn't know what to say. "When you come in the store with Michael and Alex," she said cautiously, "I would like to be able to talk to them."

"That's fine," Susan said. "That would be okay with me."

Her sudden change of heart surprised Tiffany. But we were too far gone in enjoying each other's company to be suspicious of Susan. As summer changed to fall, we spent more and more time together, alone and with my boys.

At the end of September of 1994 I was served with Susan's divorce papers. It was like being slapped in the face. We had an understanding, she and I, that we were getting a simple divorce based on our one-year separation without any specific causes mentioned.

Tom White, Susan's divorce attorney, had the papers served to me at home. I had just pulled a third shift at Winn-Dixie and was sound asleep when I heard someone knocking on my door.

You can't refuse a divorce subpoena when it's served on you like that. The guy who presented the subpoena was a private investigator hired by Tom White and Susan.

I sat there reading through the subpoena, not believing what I was seeing, flipping through the pages and wondering, "Well, what the hell is all this?"

"During the course of this marriage," I read, "defendant has carried on, and continues to carry on, an adulterous relationship with a paramour known to Plaintiff . . ." Susan was seeking a divorce "based upon the statutory grounds of adultery."

When I called her, angry at what I considered a betrayal of our agreement, she said, "I can't talk to you about it."

It took me weeks to get through to her, to finally get her to talk about it. I asked her how she could have sued for adultery. What grounds did she have that would hold up in court?

"I had a PI follow you all," she said, meaning a private investigator. It was the same guy who had served me with the papers.

There was a trace of smugness in Susan's voice. Now it began to make sense, why Susan had started acting so sweet with Tiffany in the past month. She was setting us up, encouraging us to see each other so the PI could catch us in the act.

I actually read the private investigator's report sometime later. I found it in Susan's purse when I went in there to fetch her checkbook. I read the first sentence, figured out what it was, then folded it up and put it in my pocket. It's a spooky thing, to read something written by someone who was observing you while you didn't think anyone was watching. It made me angry that Susan had sunk that low.

What about all our talk about settling this whole thing on an agreeable basis? Now I was being made out to look like some kind of weasel.

I just blew up when I first read the divorce papers. I called Tiffany and screamed at her.

"Stay away from me! I don't want to see you any-more!"

I was through with it. All the fooling around I was doing had landed me in deep trouble. I was going to go down as an adulterer. Even though it was technically the case, I knew that the truth was more complicated than that.

Susan was guilty, too. I knew that Susan had stepped out on me first, and more frequently, and with many more lovers than I'd ever had. I knew she had lied and manipulated me.

And yet she had accused me of adultery. Tiffany and I were the ones who were going to get our names dragged through the mud. It wasn't fair.

After I cooled down some, I naturally turned to Tiffany to discuss what we should do.

"Just get the divorce," Tiffany told me. "I don't care

how you get it. Let her get us for adultery. I don't care. I'll get a name for a while, but I'll get over it. I don't care what people think. I want to be with you.''

Tiffany could take the high road, but I wasn't so sure that was the way to go. I began to think about the possibility of exposing Susan as having affairs, too. I knew that if we tried to catch her at her own game, we could do it fairly easily. I knew what she was like. I knew her ways. I had already caught her in numerous lies during our marriage. I had a buddy who was a PI himself, and he said he would follow her if I wanted. So I knew if we decided to do it, it would only be a matter of time.

I reread those divorce papers. "No, this is wrong," I said. It was wrong for Susan to slam me for doing what she herself was guilty of at that very same moment.

Despite portraying herself as an angel in her divorce papers, Susan wasn't exactly acting like one. For one thing, she had started to spend a lot of time at Hickory Nuts, Union's only bar. It had just opened during the summer.

I suppose a lot of the pastors in town must have labeled this place a den of sin, if only because it was the first place in town anyone could sit and nurse a beer. I was in it once when it opened and it seemed tame enough to me. Just a big old bin of a place, with a dance floor up front, pool tables along the sides, and a raised bar in the middle.

To Susan, though, Hickory Nuts seemed to represent an opportunity to turn herself into some sort of a honky-tonk girl. The folks from Conso went there a lot after work, and she started going with them. The only other time I was in the place, apart from that first check-it-out visit, was once when I had to go there to remind her that she was expected home to pick up the boys.

We had arranged that Susan would come to my apartment to get Michael and Alex by nine o'clock. When it got to be ten and I hadn't heard from her, I started to get a little worried—and a little angry. I got a friend to watch the kids while I ran over to Hickory Nuts.

Susan was drinking with a group of Conso people. I wasn't too popular with them. They always were of the opinion that Susan could do better than me. Tom Findlay was there, but he wasn't sitting with her. She was with Donna (who also worked at Conso) and Mitch. I made Susan come outside with me.

"What's going on?" I said.

"I'm just finishing my drink."

"Don't you remember that you have to pick up the boys?" I asked.

"Yeah, but I just got caught up socializing," she said. She never did apologize.

Susan was sending me mixed messages. Half the time she was cold as ice, barely even talking to me when I picked up the boys or dropped them off after spending time with them.

Sometimes, though, especially when she had been drinking at Hickory Nuts, she threw herself at me, doing everything in her power to lure me back into her bed.

"Susan, I've got to go," I said one evening. She had been at Hickory Nuts while I had stayed at Toney Road, putting the boys to bed and watching television. Now she was acting playful.

"Come on," she said.

I could smell beer on her breath. I took a couple of steps back from her, and she followed right along. She started to undo her blouse.

"Susan, Susan . . . I don't want to."

"Yes, you do," she said, and dropped her bra. "Can't you stay a little while?"

It was true that her body was in the best shape it had been in since Michael was born. She had started going to aerobics classes and lost all the weight she had picked up. I was only human, and she was looking real good. Despite all that, I managed to say goodnight and get out of there.

Other nights, I wasn't so strong. There were a few times during those months when Susan and I went to bed together. Sometimes we didn't agree—she said yes and I said no, or it was the other way around. But on two or three occasions that fall we were both in the mood at the same time, and one thing led to another—divorce or no divorce.

It made me feel more confused than ever. Here we were, warring over our divorce yet sleeping together. She was hard to resist sometimes. As I said, Susan was a real hunk of hell, and she knew it.

In the middle of October—just a few days before the boys disappeared and my world caved in—Susan came home from a night of drinking at Hickory Nuts.

I was there, taking care of the boys. She kind of baited me again, changing her top in front of me, acting sexy. We both laid down as we usually did, on the floor with Michael between us, so he could go to sleep.

Susan had drank so much that she soon fell asleep herself. I got up to go into Winn-Dixie. Seeing her purse on the table, I couldn't resist looking in it.

I found a letter from Tom Findlay. He had typed it on his computer and the date on the top read October 17, 1994.

As I read it, I grew more excited as I saw what I had found. It was a letter from Findlay to Susan, supposedly breaking off the relationship. It gave me written proof that the two of them had an affair.

Tom began the letter by telling Susan how much he liked and admired her. "You'll make some man a great wife," he wrote. But then he told Susan that it wasn't going to happen between them. "We're too different," Findlay wrote. "We have different backgrounds."

There was another thing holding him back, Findlay wrote. The children. He didn't want a ready-made family. He didn't know if he even wanted a family at all.

Then Findlay gave some information on his romantic history in Union, how he fell for this girl or that girl like "a ton of bricks." Findlay then wrote that he was "not mad at [Susan] for what happened this weekend," filling in some details about her fooling around with another guy.

The Findlay letter was exactly what we needed: proof that Susan had had an adulterous affair. It would be enough to get Findlay to testify in a divorce proceeding, where he would be under oath.

Now that I had the evidence, though, I didn't know what to do with it. Susan was out cold, sleeping next to Michael. She snored softly, as she usually did when she went to sleep after a night out drinking.

Somehow, I had to get the letter copied and get it back into Susan's purse without her knowing that I had taken it.

It was night, and there weren't any late-hours copy shops in Union.

I raced into work with the letter and talked to Tiffany, who was just getting off her shift.

"Come here, quick," I said to her, dragging her off into a corner of the back room. "Look at this."

Tiffany read it.

"I've got to get copies made tonight somehow," I told her. "I've got to get this thing back into her pocketbook before she knows it's gone."

Tiffany thought for a minute, then remembered there was a copy machine in the office of her church. Her mother was a secretary there.

"I'll take it to church and get some copies run off," Tiffany said. So she drove home, got her mother's keys, and went and used the church copier. It was spooky, she said, being alone in the big dark church at midnight, with just the light of the copy machine.

The next morning I told Susan I'd come over and take the kids, and she was more than happy to agree. While she was in the shower that morning, I slipped the letter back into her purse, and she never knew that I had taken it.

Even in the midst of all this, we still had to act like a family. One of the last real times we had together, the boys and Susan and I, was when we visited the Union County Fair. There was a carnival and there were a lot of 4-H animal exhibits, set up around the Union County Fairgrounds across the highway from Winn-Dixie.

We walked around for a couple hours in the evening, looking for a ride that was tame enough for Michael to go on. It was important to me to do things like this, if only for the happiness of the boys.

But I could see that Susan didn't want to be there. We passed some Conso people, who seemed to look at us disapprovingly.

''Can we go now?'' she asked, after we had been there a short time. She wanted to be somewhere else, out at Hickory Nuts, probably—anywhere but there.

But for the boys' sake, she stayed.

One time I put Michael in a kiddie car, and I thought he'd be all set. Then another kid, a little girl, came and sat down next to him, and he spooked. He got up out of that car and came running over to me.

I laughed. ''Not that one, either, huh?'' He was always a sensitive kid, still pretty shy, just learning to go out and face the world.

We finally settled on a merry-go-round. Michael sat on one horse with me, and Alex sat on a horse next to us with Susan. As we waited for the ride to start, I remember that I looked over to Susan. She was staring off over the fair, a sad and lonely look on her face. But Fat Rat looked right at me and smiled.

It was a modern carousel, not one of those slow, old-fashioned kinds, and that ride went fast. I was surprised that one or the other of them didn't start wailing, but Michael and Alex held on for dear life and we whirled around for what seemed like a very long time.

CHAPTER

FIFTEEN

A week had passed since Michael and Alex had disappeared, and my only thought was how to keep the heat on the search to find them. One sure way I knew was to use the media.

All three network morning programs—*The Today Show, Good Morning America,* and *CBS This Morning*—offered their services to broadcast our appeal. We were scheduled to go live to the country the next day, on Thursday morning.

In the early morning on Wednesday, we had another sickening disappointment. Out on the West Coast, a baby that supposedly looked a lot like Alex had been dropped off by a man at a motel. The driver's car had had South Carolina plates.

Other things the man did, like leaving the baby in the motel room for too long, made the authorities suspicious. Sheriff Wells called Beverly at around seven A.M. and told him he was going to hold a press conference about the new development. He didn't want to get our hopes up, he said, but he felt he had to tell us about this. The baby had been placed with Social Services in Seattle.

This is it, I told myself. *This is what we've been waiting for.*

Three hours later, my hopes were crushed. The man was the baby's father. He and his wife had moved to Seattle from South Carolina. I was back to the deep, dark bottom of despair once again.

We were in Susan's bedroom, alone, hiding from the world after our disappointment of the morning. I had just heard that Conso Products had offered to contribute to a reward fund for Michael and Alex. Carey Findlay and his wife had expressed their interest in the search and their concern for the boys personally.

Maybe it was my sadness or the news about Findlay, but I started an argument with Susan about her affairs at Conso. I almost couldn't help myself and it only made us both feel worse.

All this was hanging over our heads when we met with the press on the steps of the Union County courthouse Wednesday afternoon. The press conference, and the next day's appearance on the morning shows, were my way of trying to keep Michael and Alex squarely in the public eye. But it wasn't something we were looking forward to doing. "Let's get back in front of those stinking cameras again," I told Susan.

Walking out into that crowded semicircle of reporters, I got the same feeling in the pit of my stomach that I'd had whenever I'd faced the press. If I could have been any-where but there, I'd have gone in a second. But I forced myself to go through with it for my boys.

Susan didn't want to be there, either. For all her excitement about being on national TV, she dreaded every appearance before a camera. For this one, she wore her white hair bow and her glasses. She began our joint appeal.

"First of all, I would like to say to whoever has my children that they please, please, bring them back home to us, where they belong. Our lives have been torn apart by these tragic events. I can't express how much they are wanted back home, how much we love them, we miss them."

She stumbled then, not able to get the words out. "They're in our hearts . . ." she said, and then stopped, collecting herself.

"I have prayed every day. There's not one minute that goes by that I don't think about these boys. And I have prayed that whoever has them, that the Lord will let him realize that they are missed and loved more than any other children in this world. Whoever has them, I pray every day that you're taking care of them, and know we will do anything, anything, to help you to get them home, back to us. I just can't express enough that we just got to get them home. That's just where they belong, with their mama and daddy."

I had thought over what I was going to say before I stepped up to the mike, but when it was my turn to speak, it rolled out of me almost without my thinking. I just said what I felt.

"I would like to take the time to plead to the American public that you please not give up on these two little boys or the search for their safe return home to us, that you continue to look for this car, for our children, and for the suspect himself. That you continue to keep your eyes open and anything that you see that might help, to please call and let it be known.

"We ask that you continue to pray for me and my wife and for our family. But most of all, that you continue to pray for Michael and Alex, that they are returned home safely to their mother and father and the family members who love them so much. That you pray most of all for them and that they are being taken care of and that they are safe, and that they will return home safely."

I didn't know what else I could add. What I felt most deeply was the wish that people not forget the terrible predicament that Alex and Michael were in. I wanted the whole country to be thinking about them.

Susan took over to add a more personal appeal.

"I want to say to my babies that your mama loves you so much, and your daddy and this whole family loves you so much. And you guys have got to be strong, because I just know, I just feel in my heart that you're okay. You've got to take care of yourselves. And your mama and daddy are going to be right here waiting on you when you get home. I love you so much."

"We love you," I said. Susan then told a story that we had talked about before, but that I wasn't sure she'd want to share with the public.

"I want to tell a story. The night that this happened, before I left my house that night, Michael did something that he's never done before. He had his pooper [our family word for pacifier] in his mouth, and he came up to me and he took his pooper out, he put his arms around me and he told me, 'I love you so much, Mama.' He's always told me he loved me, but never before, not without me telling him first. And I'm holding on to that so much, because it means so much.

"I love them. I just can't express it enough. I have been to the Lord in prayers every day with my family, by myself, with my husband. It just seems so unfair that somebody could take two such beautiful children. And I don't understand. I have put all my trust and faith in the Lord, that he's taking care of them, that he will bring them home to us.

"That's all I want to say . . ."

I was so overwhelmed by what Susan had said and the emotions behind it that I loved her more at that moment than I ever had before. *If anything can get people thinking about my boys, that will do it,* I thought. Susan had successfully answered all the people who had had the gall to say she'd had something to do with Michael and Alex's disappearance.

Later, after we were in private again, I covered her face with kisses, thanking her.

My dad and stepmom were always advising me to take a break from the Russells' house and stay with them at Toney Road for a night.

On Wednesday evening, after the press conference, I told them I would take them up on it. I'd had a blow-out with Susan back at her mama's house—our first fight since the boys had disappeared.

The fight was about the way my family was being treated at the Russells'. My mother isn't the easiest person to get along with, and that evening Linda actually wound up yelling in Mom's face.

It was a mess. My mother left crying, I lashed out at Susan, and we argued. I took off down Heathwood Road on foot. Susan jumped into a girlfriend's car and the two of them took off after me, with Susan trying to persuade me through the window to get in the car and come back to the house.

I finally relented, but that night I told Susan I was going over to visit with my dad for a while.

I was surprised by what I saw when I got to Toney Road. That afternoon, the police had searched the house for evidence. They had done so before, of course, but this was a thorough combing through for evidence. Susan and I had given our permission. I was certain they wouldn't find anything, but if it would allow them to narrow the focus of their search, it was worth it.

The yellow ribbon was still there, wrapped around the front railing. I walked inside and was hit with a blast of nostalgia for my life with the boys. I walked into Michael's bedroom, sat down on his bed, and looked around at the familiar toys and clothes strewn around. I just stayed there for a long time, thinking about Michael and Alex, even though I knew my dad and stepmom and Uncle Doug were waiting for me outside in the living room.

My Uncle Doug, my father's older brother, had come to Union that Tuesday afternoon, driving down from his home in Michigan. Later he said he never actually knew what had moved him to come. The family was in need, of course, and Doug is a good-hearted, generous man.

Everything in the house had been covered with a fine graphite dust, fingerprint dust, black and dirty. The doorways, drawers, tables, kitchen countertops, Michael and

Alex's toys, the bathroom fixtures—everything. It was incredible. If someone was trying to make the house unlivable, they couldn't have done a better job. Every time you touched a surface, your fingers would come back with some of the sootlike powder on them.

In the middle of this were my Uncle Doug, my father, and my stepmom. They would all spend the day at the Russells' with the rest of us, or sometimes at the National Guard, if Susan was being questioned there, but they would go back to Toney Road at night. My dad and stepmom slept in the bed Susan and I had shared. Uncle Doug slept on the sofa. No one stayed in Michael and Alex's rooms.

We chatted a little, while I looked around at the mess the SLED folks had left. It depressed me to see Michael's plastic workbench, the one we had given him last Christmas, covered with a thin film of fingerprint dust. Everyone was eager to have me eat dinner and sleep there, but I was already getting antsy.

"I know I told you all that I was going to stay," I said, "but I've got to get back to Linda's." Something might happen, I told them. They might find the boys, and I wanted to be with Susan when they did.

The weather had been picking up that day and the day before, and as I left Toney Road I remember the yellow ribbons flapping in the wind.

When I got back to the Russells' at around midnight, Susan was waiting. I was just thankful that she was there.

"Where've you been?" she asked, when I came in the door. "I'm glad you're back."

"Everything okay?" I asked. Susan nodded and we went to bed.

We were up early on Thursday. All the furniture had been shoved out of the living room at the Russells'. They needed the space to make room for the news crews.

Susan and I were going to take our case live to the nation. *Today, CBS This Morning,* and *Good Morning, America* had all sent people. They set Susan and me up on a couch, facing a camera and a bank of lights. We sat there and waited for the red signal light to come on atop the camera. That would mean we were being beamed into millions of America's homes.

All three shows were using the same set-up, so we did them assembly-line style, one after another. The first two were taped, at six-fifteen and six-forty-five, but the third was live, at a little after seven in the morning. As soon as we started, I realized it was all a mistake.

The interviewers—I think Harry Smith of CBS was up first—zeroed in on the question of Susan's guilt. Instead of, "Where are the boys?" what the networks were interested in was, "What does Susan know about their disappearance?"

Susan was calm and direct, answering their charges.

"I don't think any parent could love my children more than I do, and I would never even think about doing anything that would harm them. The truth has been told. I know what the truth is and I did not have anything to do with the abduction of my children.

"It's painful to have the finger pointed at you when it's your children. Whoever did this is a sick and emotionally unstable person. I can't imagine why anyone would want to take our children.''

She referred to the brief sunny period when we'd thought Alex had been located in a motel in Seattle.

''I was running around my house yesterday morning all excited. I really thought they had found one of my children. And when I got to the courthouse and found that lead had disintegrated, I was very devastated.''

She kept coming to how awful it was to be linked to her own sons' disappearance.

''It hurts to know that I may be accused. I do not understand why they would do what they are doing. Our lives have been torn apart by this tragic event. I can't express how much they are wanted back home.''

They hit me with a direct question: Did I think Susan was involved in the boys' disappearance?

I said what I felt. ''I believe my wife totally.''

On NBC's *Today* show, the questions were only a little softer. They allowed Susan to paint a picture of the anxiety she had been experiencing.

''I was thinking last night, as a mother, it's only a natural instinct to protect your children from any harm, and the hardest part of this whole ordeal is not knowing if your children are getting what they need to survive. And it hurts real bad to have that protection barrier broken between parent and child.

''But I have put my faith in the Lord, and I really believe that He's taking care of them. And they're too beautiful and precious that He's not going to let anything happen to them.

"And Michael and Alex, I love you. And we're going to have the biggest celebration when you get home."

Despite her upbeat words, Susan and I were both depressed and frustrated after these appearances. I had wanted to use the media, and now I was the one who felt used by them. All the reporters seemed to want to do was to smear Susan.

We were supposed to have another "exclusive" interview that afternoon, with the local newspaper, the *Union Daily Times*. The reporter had been following the story from day one, and the photographer was the same one who'd taken our photo the night the boys had disappeared.

Susan and I begged off. After getting up early that morning to get put through the wringer on national television, all we felt like doing was going back to her bedroom and being alone.

She slept some, but I was too full of adrenaline.

At noon, Susan got up to leave the house. She had been asked to bring a paper she'd filled out to Mr. Logan, the SLED polygraph expert. It was her written account of everything that had happened the night of the carjacking.

A SLED agent was supposed to pick her up at the Russells'. She'd just be gone a little while, they said. Susan would meet Mr. Logan coming up toward Union from Columbia, South Carolina, at a halfway point—the meeting was for some reason going to be held at the parking lot of a grocery store.

I knew the place. It was only about thirty minutes away. Susan would meet with the guy, drop off the statement, then come back.

The SLED people asked if I wanted to come along, but I

said no. My father and stepmom were at the Russells', and my Uncle Doug was planning to return to Michigan. Since I had promised to stay with them the night before but had wound up leaving, I wanted to make it up to them by spending time visiting with them.

Susan and I ducked out the back of the Russell house, avoiding the cameras set up in front. We cut across the backyard and headed to where the SLED agent waited in his car. I gave Susan a quick kiss on the mouth and waved as she drove away.

It was going to be a quiet afternoon. I was still hopeful of some big news about finding Michael and Alex, but otherwise I was content just to be with my family.

CHAPTER

SIXTEEN

M onday, the day before the boys disappeared, we resumed our routine of tracking Susan, hoping to get material for my divorce countersuit charging her with adultery. This time I was the one who followed her.

It was one more evening when Susan doffed off Michael and Alex on someone else. She had gone to her best friend Donna's house and dropped Michael and Alex there. When I picked up her trail, she was at Hickory Nuts. I noticed that Tom Findlay's car was in the Hickory Nuts parking lot also, and I assumed he was meeting Susan there.

I was with a buddy of mine, and we waited. After a while, we saw Susan come out, alone. I ducked down below the dash as Susan drove past us. We followed as she returned to Toney Road. I couldn't figure out what she was doing. Had she forgotten the boys were at Donna's? When Susan came out of the house a moment later, she had changed into her aerobics clothes. Only then did she drive to Donna's to pick up the boys.

Suddenly I realized what Susan was doing. She had told

Donna she was going to her aerobics class, and instead had driven to Hickory Nuts. This was a new level of Susan dealing with her duties as a mother. She was lying to her friends just to get a little time down at the local saloon.

The next day was Tuesday, October 25. Tiffany had the day off, and I was working the second shift.

"I'm just going to follow her again today," Tiffany told me. "Just to see what she does when she gets off work."

I said, "If you want to, that's fine." I didn't want to push Tiffany too hard in that direction or get her involved in anything she didn't like, but I wanted to catch Susan with Tom, as she did.

Tiffany was driving her mama's car so as not to raise Susan's suspicion. She first passed by Conso at around five o'clock. Susan had already gotten off work. She was sitting in her Mazda with another person, whom Tiffany could tell from the silhouette was a female. The Paradise Home Center was right across the street from the Conso parking lot, so Tiffany pulled in there to watch.

Susan sat in the Conso lot for about ten minutes. Then she pulled out and drove to Buffalo to the nursery to pick up Michael and Alex. Tiffany again followed, parking at Andy's restaurant. The lot there overlooked the Cathcarts' house, where Michael and Alex had daycare.

When she left the nursery with the boys, Susan turned left at the stoplight onto Duncan Bypass, as if she were heading back to Toney Road. Tiffany was going to give up then, but she decided to follow a little longer. To her surprise, Susan turned into the lot at Hickory Nuts.

With the boys in the backseat, Susan stopped in front of

the bar and had a conversation with one of her Conso co-workers. As Tiffany watched, the woman leaned in the passenger-side window and spoke to Susan for a while.

Something's up, Tiffany thought. *She's making plans with this girl to keep the kids tonight, so that she can go out with Tom.*

Susan then pulled out of the lot and drove back toward town.

"Now where's she going?" Tiffany asked herself.

It was just by chance that Tiffany saw Susan with Tom Findlay that evening. She had lost the Mazda in traffic and glanced over as she was passing the Conso plant. Susan and Tom were there, parked door-to-door in the Conso parking lot.

Tiffany came running into Winn-Dixie and dragged me aside. "She's up at Conso, talking to him in the parking lot there," she said, breathless. "What do you want me to do?"

"Just keep watching them," I said.

"I need a hat or something," Tiffany said. "So I can get close and she won't recognize me." We looked for a hat in the sunwear section but couldn't find one that fit her right.

When Tiffany got back to Conso, Susan and Tom were gone. Tiffany drove over to Toney Road and got there in time to see Susan get out of the car and go into the house. Michael was carrying the diaper bag, and Susan was balancing Alex on her hip.

It was around six o'clock. Tiffany called me at Winn-Dixie to see what I wanted her to do. Should she wait outside the house to see if Susan would leave?

"I don't think she's going anywhere," I told her. "She's probably in for the night."

Tiffany had jotted down the plate number of the woman's car in the Hickory Nuts lot. I had a buddy, a police officer in Union, who'd told me if I ever needed a tag run on an automobile, he'd do it. He wasn't supposed to, of course, but he'd do it as a favor for me. I got him to call me at Winn-Dixie and gave him the plate information. He said that it was the car of a man I knew, a Conso worker.

That didn't put us any closer to figuring out what Susan was up to that night, but it was clear that something was going on. I decided to call Susan myself.

When she answered, I immediately noticed there was something off in her tone. I heard Michael and Alex crying and screaming in the background.

"What's wrong, Susan?"

"Nothing," she said.

I asked her about the guy whose license plate we had run. "I wasn't talking to him," Susan said. She admitted she'd had a conversation at Hickory Nuts with her female co-worker, but that was it. I didn't want to push her too hard on the subject of Tom Findlay, because I didn't want to put her off. I was trying to figure out what she had planned.

"Are you cooking tonight?" I asked her. Michael and Alex started up crying in the background again. She still sounded strange to me.

"What's wrong?" I asked her again. "Something is—something's wrong."

"No, nothing."

"Come on, Susan, I know you, and I know when something's wrong. Talk to me about it."

"Well, yeah," she said, "something's sort of fucked up." She didn't say anything for a while. "But it's nothing I can talk to you about." Susan said she'd call me back in a while, and I told her that would be okay.

Then I hung up on her and went back to work. I had some stocking to do, and I started right in on it. That was around six-thirty.

Tiffany drove past the Toney Road house once more, around seven-thirty, and it was getting dark. The bedroom light was on, and the car was parked in the carport, just as it had been earlier. Tiffany concluded that Susan was indeed in for the night. She went over to the house of a friend who lived in the neighborhood and played with her friend's kids for a while, maybe forty-five minutes.

When she went by the house again, at a little before eight-thirty, the bedroom light was off and the Mazda wasn't there anymore.

Susan had gone out.

Tiffany immediately came to see me at Winn-Dixie, of course. "David, she's not home. Where do you think she is?"

"I have no idea," I said. But there were only a few places Susan was likely to go, so we decided Tiffany would head out to look for her again.

For the next hour, Tiffany drove around town, searching for Susan. She went to Linda's, to Wal-Mart, to Hickory Nuts, to Toney Road, and back again to Winn-Dixie.

She never thought of John D. Long Lake.

CHAPTER

SEVENTEEN

I heard about Susan's confession just like the rest of the world, from a report on television. I was at the Russells'. Susan still hadn't come back from dropping off her written statement with the SLED agent, and I was beginning to wonder what had happened to her. My Uncle Doug had just left to start his drive north to Michigan, and my dad and stepmom had left at the same time, to drop off a minivan they'd borrowed from a friend across town.

It was actually pretty quiet around the house that Thursday afternoon, nothing much to do but tune in to the news and wait. At about four-fifteen, there was a news flash on the radio.

"We have unconfirmed reports that Susan Smith has confessed to the killing of her sons . . .''

I didn't know what was going on. "What the hell are they talking about?'' I hadn't heard a word from the sheriff.

Minutes later, news of the confession came on television. My head was swimming. Why hadn't we heard anything officially?

Everyone in the house was now in the living room, gathered around the TV set. There was a tense buzz in the air. My dad and stepmom came back from delivering the van. They had heard the news.

"David, what's going on?" my father said.

"I don't know," I said.

Finally, the sheriff came on television himself. "Susan Smith has been arrested and charged with two counts of murder in connection with the deaths of her children, Michael, three, and Alexander, fourteen months."

Oh, God.

I just blew out of the house.

I didn't know where I was running to. Somewhere to a world where moms don't kill their kids, I guess. Waves of blackness, sorrow, rage. I had nausea in the pit of my stomach, a sickening feeling that I had never felt before.

Michael and Alex. My world had stopped turning. The two people I loved most on the face of God's earth were gone. That's when the shock kicked in. I knew they were dead.

I wound up standing in the middle of a little patch of pine woods at the edge of Mount Vernon Estates. There were needles deep on the ground and spiderwebs slung through the air. I didn't remember how I'd gotten there.

My dad had chased after me, trying to get me to stop.

"David!" he called, wheezing. "I'm out of breath. You're going to kill me. You don't need another one dead."

"I'm over here," I said. He came to get me, gently shepherding me back to the place I didn't want to go, back to people, to the house, to Linda and Bev.

"Come on," he said.

"It's not true," I said.

"David, let's just go back to the house and find out what's true and what's not true."

By then I heard the *whump-whump-whump* of the sheriff's helicopter coming out of the sky. The big light from the helicopter lit up the lawn around us, making everything shadowy and harsh.

I didn't want to have anything to do with anyone from Susan's family, of course. I don't remember anything but bits and pieces.

The sheriff's helicopter landed in the yard of Bev and Linda's neighbor. Sheriff Wells had finally gotten around to informing the family. He had waited to come until he had sent divers out to confirm that what Susan had said was true, that my boys were in the bottom of John D. Long Lake, where she had put them that Tuesday night nine days previous.

When he walked into the Russell house, the sheriff just stopped and announced the news to a room full of people, many of them virtual strangers to me.

"Susan Smith . . . has confessed . . ." He didn't have to say anything more. Everyone knew what he was talking about. "We have got the bodies."

The sheriff did not even have the courtesy to take me aside and tell me privately what had happened, as the next of kin, as the father of Michael and Alex.

Sheriff Wells might win awards for his handling of the case, but to this day I have not forgiven him for not breaking the news to me personally, alone. It was the least that courtesy—not to mention charity—demanded. I had to find out my wife murdered my sons from a TV set.

In a daze, I followed my father to the back of the Russell house. Linda and Beverly were sitting in the swing on the sunporch.

Linda turned and gave me a look. She raised her hands in a slow-motion, palms-up shrug.

"What do you want me to say?" she asked.

All I wanted to do was leave, run, escape. I hated that house. The Russells had mistreated me and my family, and I was ready to go. With the press crowding in, I asked for a police escort back to my apartment.

The sheriff had already lifted back up into the sky. The deputy said he would have to check. He got back to me and said he couldn't help me out.

It was bedlam. There were thirty, forty, fifty reporters outside the Russells', more every minute. I could see that the deputy didn't want to leave the Russells. Bev and Linda were going to get police protection, but I couldn't.

"What the hell do you think you're doing?" my step-mom said to the deputy. "You mean to tell me you want to protect these people whose daughter just confessed to murdering our grandsons, and you won't protect the father of those babies? All we want to do is leave this damn dump!"

"We don't have the manpower," the deputy said. "The sheriff says we don't have the manpower." My dad and stepmom scooped up all the clothes of mine they could find and we left.

We toughed out the reporters. My dad and I headed into the swarm. There were lights trained on the house, big boom lights. It was a battle just to get out the driveway. We drove out of the yard the back way, over the lawn. We had reporters on foot chasing us, running behind with cameras trained on the car.

"David, David!" They yelled. They were shouting other things, but I couldn't hear what. I couldn't think of anything but my sons' deaths. I didn't want anybody. My dad was sobbing himself. I didn't want anyone to comfort me. I just wanted to be alone. It had been twelve days since I had seen my boys.

We made it to my apartment with a whole train of reporters following us. My stepmom and Dad went back to the Russells' to get the rest of my clothes. I hadn't been inside ten minutes—pacing the floor like crazy, just totally lost—and then the swarm was back. There was nobody from the sheriff's office there to stop them.

"David, David, open the door!" Pounding, breaking my front door down. "We know you're in there! How do you feel about your wife's confession?"

There was no peace for me anywhere.

We had a game, Michael and I, that we played again and again in the months before his death.

We would be sitting around, playing with Alex, and I would start it up.

"He's my brother, and I love him," I'd say, pointing to Alex.

Michael would get a mock-serious look on his face. "No, Daddy," he'd shout, "he's *my* brudder, and *I* love 'm!"

"He's *my* brother, and I love him," I'd say, shaking my head. And Michael would come right back.

We'd go back and forth maybe a dozen times, Michael eventually bubbling over with laughter at the impossible idea that Alex could be his daddy's brother.

"He's *my* brudder, and *I* love 'm!"

For what seems now an endless time over those nine days, I had a simple faith that God would protect my sons. He would let nothing bad happen to Michael and Alex.

When it turned out they had drowned in the waters of John D. Long Lake that night, my faith had to change. I now had to believe that He was watching over them in death, and that they didn't suffer before they died. He put them into a deep sleep and took their lives before they hit the water. My faith tells me this is so.

They loved each other, my sons, and Michael always tried to look out for his little brother.

CHAPTER

EIGHTEEN

From the moment I heard about Susan's confession, there's been a blank, empty space that I barely remember.

I know there was a memorial service. I know there was a funeral. I replay the awful scene of sitting at the funeral home, hearing about the shape that my sons' bodies were in after spending nine days at the bottom of John D. Long Lake.

I see pictures now that were taken during those first few days. There's the white coffin, there are the crowds of mourners. There's me, out of my mind in grief, my face wracked with an anguish so deep that it amounts to physical pain. My dad and my stepmother hold me up because my legs have given way.

I know Tiffany came to me right away, and my father and stepmother stayed with me. My Uncle Doug got as far north as Knoxville, Tennessee, heard the news of Susan's confession on his car radio, and then turned around and drove back to Union.

I know it all happened, but to me, this time is just shattered fragments, images, little pieces of the puzzle.

My sons were gone. That was unbearable, but it turned out there were further trials in store for me, hurt piled upon hurt, the nightmare deepening still more. I would get on my feet and achieve some sort of shaky balance, and then a new fact about the boys' deaths would pull the rug out from under me again. Pull the floor out from *under* the rug.

It wasn't until later that Thursday night that I found out the facts of my boys' drowning. Before that, I knew they were dead, but I didn't know precisely how they had died. Sheriff Wells came in and gave me most of the facts then. He also noticed that the reporters were still lurking about my apartment. Then and only then did he detail a deputy to keep them away.

Mostly, I just drifted around my apartment in a daze. I was restless, unsettled. I would sit down in a chair and want to get right back up again. I couldn't get comfortable. I'd talk to people, then I would want to be alone. I'd go to my room, and I'd feel like I had to get out and talk.

The telephone circuits in Union were jammed. You could not get a call in or out. Everyone in town was talking about what had happened. The phone in my apartment would ring again as soon as you hung it up. After a few days of that, Uncle Doug and I finally went out to Wal-Mart and bought an answering machine.

Most of the first night I stayed locked away from everybody. I was just trying to understand, but nothing made sense.

My dad was there, and he was raging. There was never a doubt in his mind that the only thing to do was to execute

Susan for the murder of his grandsons. In a way, Dad's anger quieted mine. I felt confused and had a hundred different emotions toward Susan. But the one thing I did not want was to listen to people run her down. For some reason, that was painful to me.

So we formed a small outpost there, in my apartment, the grievers for Michael and Alex. There were two bedrooms but only one full-sized bed in my apartment, so by right of seniority, Doug got it. Dad and Susan slept on the floor in Alex's room next to his crib while Tiffany and I slept on the couch.

I cried. It was good to feel Tiffany's arms around me, but I was so far out of my mind with sadness, the rest of my emotions were closed down, and I couldn't really react.

Nothing helped, nothing soothed my grief. But there would be further pain.

Friday I went with my family to meet the Russells at the Holcombe Funeral Home, to arrange a burial for Michael and Alex. Mr. Holcombe had handled Danny's burial, and he was also the town coroner.

Tiffany and I had chosen two outfits for the boys to wear in their coffin. They were brand-new and had never been worn. Susan had bought them a couple of weeks before, and they were still in their wrappings.

I wanted to bury Michael and Alex next to Danny. I didn't care where the funeral was held, I didn't care what the pastors would say over my sons' grave. The one wish I had was that they would be buried right beside Danny in the cemetery at the Bogansville Church.

We were in one of the parlors of the big white funeral home, which was near downtown.

Linda was there, and Beverly, Scotty, his wife Wendy, my mother, my dad, my stepmom and my Uncle Doug. I looked around the room. My dad was still in his all-out rage mode. Beverly looked like he was in shock. He was in very bad shape. He looked somehow deflated, and his face was like ash. Linda was brittle, the same as ever.

It was awkward, difficult, seeing the Russells again. But I was too numb for anger.

Mr. Holcombe spoke for a while, discussing details of the arrangements. My father finally said, ''Where are the babies?''

''They're here,'' Mr. Holcombe said. Michael and Alex were in the building.

''Can we see them?''

There was an awkward silence.

Mr. Holcombe stood up and motioned to my Uncle Doug, asking if he could see him alone.

''Mr. Smith, you can't see them,'' Mr. Holcomb told Doug. ''Those babies are in sealed bags. They've been in the water for nine days. There's no way that they should look at them. I strongly recommend a closed casket.''

My uncle came back and told us, and it really hit me hard. A closed casket. Never to look at my boys' faces or touch their little hands again. Just gone.

I bolted over to the other side of the room.

Mr. Holcombe talked about what was known about how the boys had died. The autopsy showed that there were no bodily injuries, he said.

My dad asked, "Were they alive? Were they alive when they went into the water?"

Mr. Holcombe just nodded "Yes." My father lost it totally then.

"She didn't have the decency to kill them beforehand," my father shouted, almost beserk with pain. "She just let them drown in the water!"

I cannot believe we got through it all that day, deciding where the funeral was going to be held (Beverly and Linda wanted it out at their church, Buffalo Methodist, and I went along with their choice), which ministers would speak, who the pallbearers would be, what the coffin would be like.

I wanted my boys buried together in one casket, side by side. They didn't have a children's coffin that size, of course, and it would have taken days to custom-build one. So we decided on a white coffin with gold trim of the small adult size.

After my father's cry of anguish, the Smith side of the room didn't say much during the rest of the meeting. Beverly more or less took charge, even though you could tell he was hurting.

The person who was a real rock in all this was my Uncle Doug. For someone who was basically a stranger to me—a blood relative, of course, but someone who I had been allowed to see only once or twice before this in my life—for someone like that to put out all the effort he did was extraordinary.

I don't know how I could have gotten through this time without him. It was Doug who got up in front of the Union courthouse that afternoon, standing beside Margaret Gregory and my sister, Becky, to speak to the press and plead for everyone's prayers and understanding.

Uncle Doug spoke for only a few minutes that day, giving a simple statement.

Margaret Gregory spoke for a much longer time.

I felt like the Russell family was taking over the grieving of my sons, but I was too far gone in shock to do anything about it.

Friday night, Sheriff Wells gave me a letter that Susan had written to me from where she was being held in York County Detention Center.

The letter was printed in Susan's neat hand. There was no sense of emotion in the penmanship. She could have been writing a thank-you note. She drew little hearts instead of writing out the word "heart" and underlined things she wanted to emphasize.

I'm sorry, she wrote, over and over. She said she was missing the boys. *I don't know why I did it.*

She didn't mention Tom Findlay, Tiffany, or anyone else. She stated that the grief for the boys was lying heavy on her.

I know that my life is going to be hell from here on. Finally, she complained that in the midst of everyone's sorrow, her feelings were getting lost.

Nobody gives a damn about me.

I couldn't believe it. The letter shocked me. It made me think that Susan didn't have a firm grasp of reality. I thought to myself, "What kind of person would write a letter like this after she killed her kids?"

I had the same feeling later on, when I finally saw

Susan's handwritten confession. She used the same kind of little picture hearts and underlining that she'd used in the letter to me.

It sort of dazed me, the feelings she put into it, the way she had written it. The penmanship was very neat once again, as if she was writing an ordinary letter. I couldn't grasp that.

"This is just crazy," I said to the Union County solicitor, Tommy Pope, who showed me the original copy. I thought that somehow it would be more official, with dates and times and testimony. Instead, I was looking at drawings of little tiny hearts. "What kind of confession is this?"

Later still, I heard something that Susan had told the boys before she'd sent them to their deaths. "We can't go on living like this," she'd said.

That "we" bothered me. "We" can't go on living, she'd said. But only Michael and Alex had died.

Sunday was the funeral. Saturday I had the sad job of going out to the cemetery at Bogansville to see about the grave.

There was no room in Danny's plot to bury the boys. My brother had to be moved so that they could all lie together, and my Uncle Doug kindly paid for the relocation. It was all too much for me to handle.

There was something soothing to me about being with Uncle Doug. He didn't talk much, and right now I didn't feel like speaking with anyone.

"Do you want to go out to the lake, David?" Uncle Doug asked.

I had the sense that the worst thing possible had happened to me, that nothing could make me feel any more despair than I was feeling right then. I felt the desire to see where Michael and Alex had died.

Uncle Doug and I got in his car and drove through Union. We hardly spoke at all.

It was the first time I had ever been to John D. Long Lake. Susan, I knew, had taken Michael fishing there a few times with the Garner family.

We passed Shirley McCloud's house, where Susan had used the phone to call me that night. Then Doug turned left off Route 49 down the short access road to the lake. The parking lot was jammed with cars.

As soon as Doug and I got out, we heard people talking about how Oprah Winfrey had been there that day, taping one of her shows. I saw Oprah only from a distance. There I was, the one person she would have loved to get her hands on to interview, and I was fifty feet away from her. I kept my cap pulled down over my eyes and no one recognized me—one guy walked past and did a double-take, then shook his head. Naw, it couldn't be.

We stayed up above the lake and the television crews, sitting on the grassy bank. The boat ramp slanted steeply down to the water right in front of me. There were flowers, wreaths, toys, and yellow ribbons piled on the shore, and more coming every minute. People would walk up, stand a minute, leave some remembrance. There were a lot of tears and hugging, but I was dry-eyed. I had cried myself out.

It was devastating for me to see the lake where my boys had died. It seemed so cold, so barren. Sitting there, seeing all the people and the flowers, I felt a sharp stab of pain at the lonely way Michael and Alex had passed.

I spoke to them silently. *I wish it could have been me in the water instead of you.*

I walked down to the bottom of the boat ramp, staring out over the water. Behind me, a cameraman from one of the local channels was trying to take a shot of the lake.

"Could you move, please?" he asked me.

I moved out of his way. "Sorry," I said.

"David, if you don't want me to go, I can understand," Tiffany said that afternoon, when we were getting ready to go to the memorial service. "If you want me to, I will. It's up to you."

There wasn't any question in my mind. Tiffany had been there for me, all through this ordeal. I wanted her by my side at the memorial service. I didn't care what the people of Union might say about it.

The funeral home was filled with flowers, thousands of them. It was amazing. Every room was packed solid to overflowing. They had benches set up and those were stacked with memorials. Many of the arrangements were blue, the natural color for the boys, but there were wreaths of white and red carnations, roses, lilies, just about every variation you could think of. And stuffed animals and cards.

There was another memorial at the funeral home at the same time as Alex and Michael's, for the wife of a man who had been pretty high up in Union social circles. I felt sorry for him. He ended up having to have his wife's memorial service at home. There just wasn't enough room at Holcombe Funeral Parlor.

The memorial was scheduled to begin at eight o'clock. I

had a little time beforehand alone with my boys. The coffin was closed, but I stood beside it and prayed.

Then the crowds came. Friends, relatives, people from Union, people we'd never seen before from out of town, people from North Carolina, Tennessee, Georgia. Tiffany stood beside me, and Dad, my stepmom, Uncle Doug, and my mother were also in the receiving line. The Russells weren't there, although Scotty dropped by. They had opened up their home to mourners but felt it would have been inappropriate to attend the memorial.

I shook hands with, touched, or hugged every one of those people. I was so moved that everyone had come out for Michael and Alex. The line went on and on. I don't remember much about that night. My muscles started to ache, and the next day I was actually sore from doing all that hugging.

"And who's this?" I remember one lady asking about Tiffany, pretty soon after we started.

"She's my girlfriend," I said. I could tell the lady was kind of taken aback, but I didn't care. I had never met her before, and she was probably thinking of Susan and me as a unit, from seeing us on television a lot.

Tiffany smiled gratefully at me. She had been a little stiff before that, but afterward she loosened up and was a real help to me that whole evening.

We were only scheduled to stay until ten o'clock. But it was around midnight before I finally could get away. I sneaked out a back door to avoid all the cameras that were set up outside.

My Uncle Doug took the responsibility of meeting the press that night. The media sent in a representative to ask if the family would allow any cameras in church during the funeral the next day, Sunday.

"Because of all these incredible flowers and everything," the reporter said. "We should share it with the people."

Uncle Doug and my father agreed that a single camera taping the service from the back, not anything obtrusive, would be okay. Uncle Doug called Mark Long, pastor of the Buffalo Methodist Church, where the funeral was going to be held, to ask his permission.

"Absolutely not," the Rev. Long said. "That is totally off limits. I am not going to make this into a media event."

Uncle Doug went back to the reporters and said, "Sorry, guys, you got shot down."

It was our first encounter with the Rev. Long. Personally, I had only one request for him. During the funeral service, I asked that he play a tape of "The Last Song" by Elton John. In the mail on Saturday, someone had sent me a tape with just that one song on it. It was written about Ryan White, the boy who had died from AIDS at such a young age, and it was about the love between a father and his son.

Uncle Doug made sure Rev. Long got the tape and sent the message that I had requested it be played as we left the church.

The whole day of the funeral was a blur to me. It had been sunny off and on all week, but that morning it was pouring rain. I went over to the funeral home in the morning and spent some more time alone with my boys. Barb and Walt came, Uncle Doug, and my aunts from Michigan.

I sat on a chair in front of the casket and prayed for Michael and Alex.

We went back to my apartment and got dressed. My dad, my stepmom, Tiffany, and Uncle Doug were going to ride with me to the funeral. For some reason, it was arranged that we meet at the Russells' and all go over to the church in a convoy. Just being around the house on Heathwood Road made me uncomfortable.

When we drove to the church, we had to stop in front for a long time while they got all the media people out of the way. The rain had stopped by then. The whole street was blocked with satellite trucks.

We sat in the front pew. I was so distraught that I thought I was going to pass out. There were four ministers, and the Rev. Doug Gilliand opened the service. We stood and recited the "Lord's Prayer."

When they started up the hymn "Jesus Loves Me," it was like a hammer hit me. You could hear the whole congregation give out a little moan like someone had come along and jabbed everybody there. It was too much.

The Rev. Long ended the service by telling the Bible story of the death of King David's infant son. Throughout his remarks he repeated the name "David" over and over, referring to the Biblical David. It was strange. He ended with the 23rd Psalm.

I collapsed walking out of the church. My Uncle Doug and stepmom Susan picked me up and steadied me. It's all a blur of emotion and grief. Of course I didn't notice it then, but I was told later that the Rev. Long had denied my request for "The Last Song." He'd said it would be "inappropriate."

Later, at the cemetery, I said goodbye to Michael and Alex. Not for the last time. I think because I never got to see them one last time, I am still saying goodbye to them, over and over, every day. But I bowed my head over their casket and wept.

The whole area around the grave was covered in a blanket of flowers. They were at peace. I longed to touch their fingers one more time, to brush their cheeks, hold them again.

There was no peace for me.

CHAPTER

NINETEEN

The cards and letters poured in. On the Monday after the funeral, Uncle Doug and I went down to the Union Post Office because they said there was too much mail to deliver.

We picked up one box that day, another box Tuesday, two more boxes each day on Wednesday and Thursday. It's not that impressive until you realize that each box contains a thousand pieces of mail.

It was astounding. Poems—there were hundreds of verses dedicated to Michael and Alex, and heartfelt letters of condolence and support. As Christmas came on, I got thousands of Christmas cards. There were drawings, paintings, religious tokens, keepsakes, crosses, guardian angels, medallions. There were daily masses dedicated to the boys, scholarships, memorials, donations to charities of every kind. Every conceivable way that people found to show their feelings in regard to Michael and Alex came to me via the mail.

I was staggered by it. All the letters seemed to me to be proof that my sons had touched the hearts of people all over the world. Some of the messages were truly inspiring, and they got me through some dark times.

The poems in particular were moving, and what was incredible about them is maybe 99 percent of the verses ran along similar themes. *Michael and Alex are in heaven,* the people would write, *they are in pain no more.* The poems presented a picture of the boys as happy in heaven, sometimes looking down on their father and telling him not to worry about anything. Almost always, the boys were shown as being together.

It was comforting. Although I am no longer a Jehovah's Witness, the teaching was impressed pretty deeply upon me in my early years, and I have difficulty leaving it behind. The Jehovah's Witnesses believe that there is no heaven as such, that when you die, you die, and that's all. There is no afterlife. So as far as my personal belief goes, I find it hard to have faith that the boys are happy now in the hereafter. But that does not prevent me from appreciating the sentiments written in the poems, and taking solace from the picture of Michael and Alex, playing together in heaven.

In the same way, I have dozens of crosses that people have sent me. The Jehovah's Witnesses believe that Jesus did not die on the cross, but upon the stake. Therefore I have trouble wearing a cross or hanging one in my home. I am still thankful of the thought behind the gifts, though, and I can't bear to throw away anything sent to me in Michael and Alex's name.

The kindness and generosity of total strangers is something that I will never forget. To take just one example out of so many, a couple in Georgia donated the beautiful headstone that marks Michael and Alex's grave. The husband was in the memorial stone business, and when he asked his wife what she wanted for her birthday, she told him not to get her anything, but to donate the stone for the boys.

They did the stone up fine. There is a laminated photo of Michael and Alex together. Engraved on the granite is Michael's favorite saying, "He's my brudder, and I love 'm!"

The weight of the world was sitting on my shoulders, and I felt that I just had to get away. The day after the murders, my Uncle Doug had contacted a man who would be an immense help getting me through the dark times ahead.

J. Michael Turner was an attorney in nearby Laurens who my father knew. Dad knew and trusted Mike, and I was sure that I didn't want a lawyer from Union. We began to refer all the calls from the media—and there were hundreds—to Mike Turner. His office was swamped, and eventually he brought in Marvin Chernoff, the president of what is probably South Carolina's biggest public relations firm, to help out.

These people helped form a support network in the weeks after the funeral. I met Libby Morgan, an associate of Marvin's, and she helped guide me during the coming days. She recommended a therapist for me in Columbia, and eventually I began going to counseling to help work out all my emotions.

Marvin Chernoff, Mike Turner, my Uncle Doug—they all realized that it was crucial for me to take a break from Union. The pressure from the press was enormous. They were still camped out in town, breathing down my neck for interviews. I walked down Main Street one day and was ambushed by a camera. Another reason to take a break from the town was that everywhere I went in Union there were memories, places I associated with Michael and Alex.

Marvin Chernoff offered me the use of his company's condominium on Hilton Head, the resort island off the South Carolina coast. The weekend after the funerals, Uncle Doug and I took off.

It was a good feeling, being away. Even though there was never a minute that went by when I wasn't aware of the loss of Michael and Alex, the gloom lifted just a little, enough to let me draw a breath.

Uncle Doug and I did normal things like stroll on the beach and watch *Mrs. Doubtfire* on video. The best thing about being with him was that I didn't feel as if I had to talk or make conversation or say anything at all.

On Sunday Doug and I took bikes out on the beach, riding easily downwind. When we turned to head back, however, the wind was against us, and it hit hard. We struggled mile after mile against it, neither one of us wanting to lose face by giving up. Our fifteen-minute ride turned into an hour-long struggle. Yet somehow it led me to do something I never thought I'd do again: laugh out loud. When we got to the condo, we were exhausted.

During this time, I felt I had to think clearly, but my emotions kept swamping me, getting in the way. The question that was always looming before me was what would happen to Susan. A lot of people were calling for the death penalty. The Union County solicitor, Tommy Pope, was considering the question himself, and he told me that my feelings in the matter would weigh heavily in his decision. Susan had gotten a lawyer, David Bruck, who was famous for his defense against the death penalty.

Did I want Susan to die for what she'd done to Michael and Alex?

It was agonizing just to think about, and I simply told people it was way too early for me to decide one way or another. I was still sifting through my emotions.

But there were some troubling things that I learned in the aftermath of the killings. One was that Susan seemed to know exactly where the Mazda had sunk in John D. Long Lake.

Police divers had searched the lake twice during the nine days Michael and Alex were missing, once on Thursday, October 27, and again the next Sunday. They didn't find anything, because they weren't looking in the right place. It turned out the Mazda had drifted. It bobbed like a cork in the water, moving away from the boat ramp toward the lake's manmade dam.

But on Thursday, when Susan confessed, she told the authorities exactly where they could find the car. They spotted it on the first dive.

There was only one conclusion that I could make.

Susan had watched the car as it sank.

This was too awful, too terrible to imagine. Susan waiting, seeing Michael and Alex die. If that were true, there was no doubt of something truly evil in Susan's character, something unspeakable.

Another thing troubled me about the discovery of the car. When they winched it out of the lake (the babies' bodies had already been removed), the Mazda caught on the shoreline and flipped over, right side up. When it flipped, the parking lights suddenly came on.

Strange. Had Susan intentionally left the parking lights on so that she could watch the car and make sure it sank out of sight? Again, too awful, too terrible. But what other explanation could there be?

I began to put together the pieces I hadn't seen before, back during those nine days when I believed everything Susan said was true. The Tom Findlay phone call, the Auburn sweatshirt, Susan's unwillingness to stay at Toney Road, her negativity about the boys being found.

Slowly a picture came clear of Susan: desperate over Tom Findlay. Terrified that her other affairs at Conso were going to come to light. Willing to do anything to win Tom's sympathy. Willing to do the worst thing.

Altogether, it suggested the murders were cold and premeditated. Susan hadn't just snapped in a moment of madness. She had planned the whole thing.

I didn't want to believe this was true. It was a demon I had to wrestle with. Meanwhile, the solicitor was waiting on my decision.

Did I want Susan to die?

The media pressure was so intense in the weeks following the murders that sooner or later I knew I would have to respond. Besides, because reporters had helped me so much in getting the word out about my sons during the time they were missing, I felt obligated to answer their requests for an interview.

When Uncle Doug and I returned from Hilton Head, we stopped for a meeting with Marvin Chernoff and Mike

Turner. They had been talking with producers for Diane Sawyer, Barbara Walters, Katie Couric—almost every primetime network news show. We had to decide who we wanted to conduct the interview.

I knew the tabloid television folks were ruled out. They had alienated me totally. Their ruthlessness and rudeness were phenomenal. *A Current Affair* had successfully bought my mother's participation in a series of shows. My sister, Becky, did one episode of *Inside Edition* before she realized how angry it made me.

What frustrated me most was when other people portrayed themselves as speaking for me. It was an out-and-out lie when my mother said it. She did outrageous things, like come into my apartment and take photos, personal mementos, possessions, all to turn over to the folks at *A Current Affair.*

This hurt me deeply and probably damaged my relationship with her beyond repair. The sad thing about it is that I can count on the fingers of one hand the times my mother actually saw the boys. She lived near Myrtle Beach and did not come to see us all that often. She saw Alex a grand total of twice. Yet she was using her relationship with him to make money.

Can I blame her? Yes. Do I blame her? No. Mom has never had much in life, and the amount of money those producers were dangling in front of her was just too tempting for her to resist. It is toward the producers themselves that I direct most of my anger.

The networks, however, had treated me fairly during the nine days, granting me access when I wanted to appeal to the nation about the disappearance of my sons. After much discussion and quite a few meetings—Diane Sawyer came down to Union to meet with me—I decided to talk with NBC's Katie Couric.

I was comfortable with her. She had a young child of her own. The other networks would share the interview so that no one got it exclusively, but *Dateline* would be the first primetime news show to broadcast the interview.

My main reason for going on television was just to say, "Thank you." I felt that any word of thanks I gave would be small against the huge outpouring of sympathy the boys and I had received. What could I say that would come close to the 21,000 letters, the countless prayers, the amount of time people spent searching, hoping, helping? But I felt I had to go ahead and try.

The interview as a whole was difficult for me, but Katie made it as easy as she could. She didn't press me on questions about Susan. That whole subject was too raw right then for me to talk about in public.

The only time during the interview that I felt myself come alive, though, was when we shared pictures of Michael and Alex.

It wasn't until two weeks after Susan's confession that I could drive down Main Street in Union without seeing a media satellite truck parked there.

The pressure from the press might have lessened a little, but there were other things hanging over me. Everywhere I went in town, people would point and stare. I put up with it, but it made me feel uncomfortable and self-conscious. I could never relax in public and let my guard down.

Total strangers felt comfortable coming up to me and

giving me advice. Again, just one example: a guy who de-scribed himself as a paramedic came up to me in a restau-rant in Union when I was trying to have a private dinner. Out of the blue, he said, ''You've got to learn to forgive Susan, David, else how are you going to be able to ask for-giveness for yourself?''

I appreciate that he was trying to be helpful. But I didn't ask for his comments. It's as if I no longer had any privacy at all. When I went back to work at Winn-Dixie, months after the murders, strangers would come up to me while I was on the job, to inform me just what path I should follow in life. I never blew up and said, ''Mind your own busi-ness,'' but I felt like it once or twice.

Linda Russell still came into the store. That was difficult for me. There were other places to shop in Union. I tried to put myself in her shoes, and I knew that if someone I was related had killed someone's offspring, I would do my best to avoid that person so as not to cause them undue pain.

There are a lot of good people in Union, but after the murders, I began to see that there was a lot of hypocrisy, too. Some people in Union felt like Susan Smith was one of theirs. She was a hometown girl, not a country boy, like me. I was an outsider. Her stepfather, Bev, was a member of the good ol' boy network. My daddy was a stranger from Michigan, even if we had lived in the county for over two decades.

Slowly, I saw the town get behind Susan, starting to build sympathy for her as a victim. I could not stomach it. To me, she was the farthest thing from a victim. She was a cold-blooded murderer. Where were Michael and Alex in all this? As the townspeople started speaking for Susan, asking for "forgiveness," who was speaking up for the boys?

Small things annoyed me. Rev. Long, the same pastor who'd refused to play the Elton John song, who said he didn't want the funeral to become a media event, gave over his church to Oprah Winfrey for a day to tape her show.

Sheriff Wells, the person who was closest to the investigation, let it be known he was not in favor of the death penalty for Susan.

Susan's lawyer, David Bruck, manipulated the press to paint an innocent portrait of the woman who killed my sons. Bruck went to Tommy Pope one day to ask the solicitor if he would allow some family photographs of Susan to be used at the trial for evidence. The shots all showed Susan as a loving mother, nuzzling Alex, hugging Michael.

"You want photographs?" Tommy Pope told Bruck. "I've got photographs. I'll let you show those if you let me show these." And he brought out the gruesome autopsy photos of Michael and Alex. Bruck quickly withdrew his request.

The bodies had been examined the Thursday night after they were recovered. The autopsy was done in Columbia, at the medical laboratory of the University of South Carolina there. I knew the autopsy report existed, but I wasn't ready to read it. I wasn't prepared to read what had happened to Michael and Alex in the waters of John D. Long Lake. Sometime down the road, I guess I'll ask for the report. A month, six months, a year. Or maybe never.

Even without the report, I kept hearing awful things about the shape of the babies' bodies. My dad talked to the solicitor about how the boys looked. He told me that he had seen some horrible things in his tours over in 'Nam, but the solicitor told him things that blew his mind. I tried to keep from thinking about such things, but in bad moments I always returned to them. It was like worrying a bad tooth.

There was a constant pressure on me to say what I thought about the death penalty for Susan, but I never said anything about it. I did make one decision, though. I would have to see Susan before I made up my mind whether she should go to the electric chair.

CHAPTER

TWENTY

There were a lot of reasons why I shouldn't have visited Susan in jail. Just the idea of her and me getting together was bound to create public sympathy for her. And emotionally, I didn't know whether I could handle it.

Two weeks after Susan's confession, Bev Russell called me at my apartment. He said that David Bruck, Susan's lawyer, wanted me to call him. I wasn't ready to do that. I spoke to Mike Turner, and he talked to Bruck for me. The message from Bruck: Susan wanted to see me.

I didn't know what to do. I had thought a lot about seeing Susan again. But when the real possibility came up, I actually felt faint. My heart started to beat faster. A thousand thoughts raced through my head.

I felt I had to see her. There was too much left unsaid between us. In my mind I had a sheet of questions ten miles long—some of the same questions people were asking all over the country.

I told Mike to go ahead and set up the meeting.

It was a gray, drizzling day when I went down to the

Women's Correctional Facility near Columbia about three weeks after Susan's confession. The depressing weather fit my mood. I met Mike at a Quincy's restaurant in Newberry, left my car in the lot there, and continued on to Columbia with him.

We were supposed to meet David Bruck outside the prison. As we neared the place, I felt myself getting more and more emotional. I couldn't talk. I could barely think. I felt like I was hyperventilating. The prospect of meeting with Susan was affecting me so much that all I hoped was that I wouldn't faint upon seeing her.

Bruck was parked in the lot of an abandoned restaurant, the Lizard's Thicket, which was right across the street from the prison entrance. I felt like I was in a detective novel. We got out of Mike's car and got into Bruck's brown Ford Taurus. The rain still came down. Everything was gray and depressing, like the boarded-up windows of the restaurant.

Bruck said a few short words to me about being sorry for my loss. They didn't even register. My head was buzzing and I was trying to keep myself together for the meeting.

Susan's lawyer spoke into his car phone. "Hello, this is David Bruck. We're coming in."

The whole thing had been prearranged. We signed in at the guardhouse and glided through the gates of the prison. Then it was weird—we were in the middle of a pasture. There were cattle grazing on both sides of the road. They actually had a farm there inside the prison. All the while, I was getting more and more apprehensive, until it felt like my head was going to burst.

"Are you all right, David?" asked Mike, who was sitting in the backseat. He put his hand on my shoulder. I couldn't even reply.

We parked in front of the administration building and went inside. We passed through a metal detector and then walked down a long hallway.

"Step in here," said one of the corrections officers, and when we went through the door, I was surprised to find myself in a men's washroom.

"Please take off your shoes and your jacket," the officer said. They were going to search us. It was all very polite and efficient, but it still made me feel like a criminal. I even had to open up my mouth and show them under my tongue.

We were then led across the hall through a door into a staff training room. Susan was seated inside the room.

She was facing away from me, so I saw her before she saw me. She could hear us across the room, coming toward her, but she didn't look around. She had on her denim blues, had her hair put up the way she always does. She was sitting at a table, and I crossed over to stand behind her.

Then she turned. When we made eye contact, that was it. My heart must have skipped five beats. It was breathtaking to see her, to see the murderer of my children, for the first time since she'd confessed.

I had a feeling of horror.

My hand went to my mouth involuntarily. I was forced to look away from Susan for a second. It was a gut-wrenching feeling. I was dragged way down inside, as if seeing her helped release some pain I had in me. I was afraid I was going to pass out, and I needed to take a few deep breaths before I could go on.

She broke down and started crying, and I went to her then. We hugged.

"I'm so sorry," she said.

She didn't want to let go of me. She grabbed me around the neck and kept hugging. We started to sit, and if I hadn't been holding her up, she'd have gone to the floor.

I said, "Susan, look, you've got to sit up, because I've only got an hour. We've got to talk. You've got to pull yourself together."

Mike Turner left then. David Bruck stayed for part of the hour, but then he left us alone, too.

On one whole wall, there was a glass window to the room. A van was parked in a courtyard just outside the window, pulled in with its doors open. The interior of the van was dark, and you had to look hard to notice they had a corrections officer inside the van, watching us.

I don't remember seeing any of this at the time. All I saw was Susan.

I kept asking her why. Why had she done it?

She said, "I don't know why."

"Why in the name of heaven didn't you just give the kids to me? I would have taken them."

"I know. I don't know why I didn't."

"You broke my heart," I told her. "You ripped my life away. Damn you. Damn you to hell, Susan, for what you've done."

"I'm sorry, I'm so sorry," she said, over and over.

I pulled out a little picture of our kids and showed it to her, and we cried together. "I miss them, too," she said.

I got angry at her then. I took the picture and raised it in front of her face and then brought it down on the table.

"Why?" I said. "Why . . . why . . . why . . . why?"

Slamming down the photo of my boys over and over.

She couldn't answer me.

I said, "You know, I just didn't know you cared about Tom Findlay this much."

"I didn't, either," she said, as much as admitting that he was part of the reason for what she did.

"What am I going to do, Susan? I'll never be able to show my kids how to ride a bike. I'll never get the chance to take them fishing or teach them how to play ball. You just ripped this from me."

"I'm having a hard time, too," Susan said. "Nobody cares about me down here. I'm in a little bitty cell," she said. "I don't get to go out but an hour a day."

We talked about Michael and Alex again. She asked what kind of coffin the boys had had. I told her that it was a white one with gold trim, that they had to use one for a small adult in order to bury them both together.

It had to be a closed casket, I said.

"Do they tell you the condition . . . the condition of their bodies?"

I couldn't answer her. At that time, I didn't know much myself. But I couldn't believe that Susan—the very person who'd put my boys at the bottom of a lake and then lied about it so they'd had to stay there for nine days—had had the gall to ask me that question.

Somehow, I couldn't be angry. I felt sorry for her, although my heart has hardened since. She was incarcerated;

she was wearing belly chains and ankle chains every time she left her cell.

I never asked the specific questions that had been keeping me up at night, the questions that I really needed answers for. Did she watch as the car sank into the water? How slowly did it sink? Were the kids awake? Were they crying for their mama?

I never confronted her about any of this. Somehow, I felt like I didn't want to put her through any more than she'd already been through. I didn't want to hound her. Even now, I would be lying if I said I didn't still care about Susan.

We cried a lot during that meeting, cried and hugged. It was like we were playing two roles. One role was loving parents who had just lost their kids. The other role was that Susan was the murderer of those kids, and I was the husband she'd betrayed. We kept going back and forth between those roles. I would question her and ask her why one minute. Then the next minute we'd be crying together, missing Michael and Alex.

I even wiped the tears off her face a couple times, sitting there with her. She had some crumpled-up Kleenex in her hand. I would take one and dry her cheeks with it. It was almost more emotional upheaval than I could take.

The strangest thing that happened during that meeting, the thing that chilled me the most, was something Susan said about "after we get through all this."

"David, when I get out . . . *if* I get out of here, I hope that maybe we can get back together and have more kids."

I turned away from her and couldn't speak.

She asked me a last question before they took her out: "You going to come back?"

I stood there for a second or two and I took a deep breath. I said, "Yeah, I'll come back."

She said, "You promise?"

"Yeah, I promise," I said. "I don't know when, but yeah, I promise I'll be back one day."

"Do you hate me?"

I looked away from her again, into the courtyard where the prison van was parked. She was asking too much of me.

"I don't hate you, Susan, but I hate what you did."

I gave her another hug, and then they started putting the handcuffs on her.

It was a long trip back to Union from the prison, first driving with Mike, then on my own after I picked up my car.

Mike and I didn't talk much at first. I felt like I had run a race or something. My body was limp. I was exhausted. We drove in silence. It was still raining, and the countryside looked gloomy.

When we did talk, it was about the meeting with Susan. I told Mike some of what she'd said. Then I asked him to explain the law to me again. Even though Tommy Pope and Mike both had told me about how South Carolina's death penalty works, I felt like I had to get it straight in my head.

Mike dropped me off at my car. I could tell he felt a little sorry for me, having to face that ride back to Union alone. I told him I would be okay.

What I thought about mostly, on that trip back, was the decision I had to make.

I had told myself that I wouldn't make up my mind how I felt about the solicitor going after the death penalty for Susan until I saw her again. I had wanted to base my judgment on the way she behaved about what she'd done.

When I thought back over the visit, what struck me most was that she didn't seem really sorry, despite saying she was again and again. If the roles were reversed, I would have been stretched out on the floor, wrapped around her ankles, bawling my head off that I was sorry, wailing for forgiveness.

It was like her written confession. If you read it, you see she doesn't talk that much about the boys. She says she's sorry a few times and that's it. Mostly it's about *Susan,* how *Susan* feels.

In South Carolina, the law holds that convicts with life sentences can be paroled after twenty years. One thing I was certain of was that that was not long enough. In twenty years, Susan would still be of childbearing age. Susan didn't deserve another chance at her freedom. Who knows who her next victims would be—her kids? Another family member? A total stranger?

I knew I didn't want her out to live a free life again. The only way to make absolutely certain she never had freedom would be to put her on Death Row.

On that drive back home, I went round and round with all the arguments. In a sense, execution was too good for her. What I wanted was for her to sit for the rest of her life in some blank, empty space, like the emptiness that now surrounded me, just forced to think every day about what she had done, to wake up with it in the morning and go to sleep with it at night. That's what I thought would be a fitting punishment for her.

Susan should *never* get out of prison. But a sentence of "life in prison" really means twenty years. That was the main argument in favor of the death penalty for her after she is found guilty of murdering Michael and Alex. If I didn't want her out to live a free life again, the only way to make absolutely certain she never has freedom would be to put her on Death Row.

Did I want Susan to die? In South Carolina, prisoners are put to death in the electric chair. I didn't think I had enough hatred toward her to see her executed. But if killing your babies in a cold-hearted, premeditated way didn't mean you deserved the death penalty, what crime did?

My brain was buzzing with all these thoughts by the time I got back to Union. I had to make a decision within the next few weeks. Tommy Pope had to make an announcement about whether he would seek the death penalty. It wasn't all up to me, but if I opposed his decision, Tommy would be out on a limb.

My father, of course, never had a question. Send her to the chair, he said.

I still didn't know what I wanted to do.

When I did decide, I knew it was going to be rough. The solicitor asked me to be there when he made the announcement to the press.

"You've got to back me up," Tommy Pope told me. I didn't want to go back out there in front of the cameras. But I thought if I went the extra mile for him, he would go the extra mile for me. Susan had the best representation.

David Bruck had all sorts of tricks up his sleeve. I needed Pope to be totally committed to this trial.

Bruck had already showed he was a master of strategy by revealing what Pope was going to announce the next day: that the state of South Carolina would be seeking the death penalty in the case of Susan Smith. Bruck stole Tommy Pope's thunder. He was able to shape the news as he wanted to. It was just a sign of what we would be up against in the coming trial.

But Tommy Pope had to go through with the official announcement anyway. When I stepped outside the Union County courthouse with him, it flashed back at me. There was a big crowd of reporters waiting. None of them went after him. They all gathered in front of me.

I had this awful sensation of suddenly being back there during those nine days, when I was in front of the press like that all the time. The flashbulbs, the lights, the cameras. Everyone shouting. Total chaos. It made me feel disoriented, almost as if I didn't know where I was, when it was.

Tommy Pope called the reporters back to him, saying he would make a statement before I talked. The solicitor announced that he would seek the death penalty because of the heinous nature of the crimes. He said he had the full support of the Smith family. Then he stepped back and let me say a few words.

I had a simple message. "Remember who lost their lives." That's what was getting lost in all the David Bruck maneuvering, all the news stories which were coming out about how Susan was a victim.

When I stood up there on the courthouse steps and said I supported Tommy Pope asking for the death penalty, I was really asking people to put the focus back on Michael and Alex.

They are the victims. They are the ones who died awful, unspeakable, senseless deaths, suspended upside down in their carseats, as the water seeped into the Mazda and rose over their little heads. And they're the ones who stayed in that lake while their mama lied.

If Susan succeeds in avoiding the death sentence that she deserves, if she is told she must serve just twenty years, I don't really know how I will react.

I do know one thing. I will never be able to live a full life, because I will wind up living the next twenty years for the day when she gets out. I'll always have that date in the distance to deal with. There will always be questions plaguing the back of my mind: *How am I going to react when she gets out? What am I going to do? Is she going to look me up when she gets out, hire a private investigator, and track me down, just so she can check and see how I'm doing all through the years? Find out if I've had more kids?*

I can't help but focus my next twenty years on the day she gets out. Wanting to know what I'm going to do, wanting to know what she's going to do.

If, on the other hand, I know she is locked in prison forever, then I can have a full life again. I can relax, more or less, and not have to worry about what Susan Smith is going to do.

The only way to ensure that is to put her on Death Row. If all her appeals fail and all the strategies of David Bruck and the lawyers came to naught, and if at some future date the state prepares to execute her, then I have decided I can accept that. It's not what I want. I don't want to see Susan die. But if it happens, so be it.

The Bible says it best. You reap what you sow.

CHAPTER

TWENTY-ONE

As the weeks since Michael and Alex died stretch into months, I don't think I have even started to deal with the fact that they are gone from my life forever.

Healing is a long, slow process. I don't think I'll ever be completely healed, of course. The wound is too deep. But I can sense myself changing. There are easier days, now. They're not as tough as they were.

Whereas before there were never five minutes that went by when I didn't agonize over what happened, now the time period has stretched out. Now there is sometimes a half hour, an hour, when I don't face what happened in my thoughts.

I know there is more pain ahead for me. The solicitor says that at the trial, the defense will slam me pretty hard, try anything to lay all this off on me, as if Michael and Alex's deaths are my fault.

Some things have helped. Our divorce became final in early May. It was a relief finally to be legally free of her. There was a routine court procedure to declare Susan's and my marriage dissolved. Tom Findlay testified to their adultery. Susan was not contesting the charges. She waived her right to appear.

The only difficult time I had during my short court appearance was when the lawyers asked me if the children that had come of the marriage were now deceased, and I had to say out loud that they were.

In the settlement, I got half of Michael and Alex's toys and clothing. Susan got the other half. I received the Mazda, which I will have destroyed as soon as Susan's trial is over and it is no longer needed as evidence.

Tiffany helps me a lot—as much as I let her. She is still very much in my life, and we have gone through so much together that we share a common bond. When I meet new people now, I am never sure if they are attracted to me for whatever celebrity I have or because they really like me. It's hard for me to trust people. So it's good to have someone like Tiffany, who was on my side before all this happened and has remained there all through the past few months.

As much as we can, we've tried to leave the small world of Union. I've moved to an apartment in Spartanburg, about thirty miles away. I commute to Winn-Dixie on my motorcycle.

The Thanksgiving after the boys died, Tiffany and I went up to Michigan with my dad and stepmom to visit Doug. My dad is so important to me in this time. I remember taking a walk after Thanksgiving dinner along the shoreline of Lake Michigan. With the wind chill, the air was below zero, but it was a good day. It felt right for us all to be together.

I had Tiffany take a picture of me and my dad. I hugged him for the shot, and it made me think that I never did that enough when I was growing up. Tell him how much I loved and admired him. Throw my arms around him and show him that I did.

The counseling that I got helped a lot. It eased me through the real immediate jolt of the boys' deaths. My counselor and I talked about how I closed myself off emotionally in the wake of the murders.

What I have to do now is learn to live again. I realize I still have a long row to hoe. I know I haven't even really begun to put my life back together. I haven't really had a chance even to grieve, to sit down and go through this pain, suffer through it, get it out of my system somewhat.

I thought moving to Spartanburg would make a difference. It helped for a little while. But then the benefit seemed to wear off and the pain returned. I thought a lot of things would help me. I bought a new motorcycle, because I love to ride, and I thought that would give me a second wind. But it hasn't helped any.

There still aren't any good days. Probably one reason why I'm not doing any better than I am is because I won't let anybody help me out. Tiffany pleads with me. Because of everything that's happened, though, my system can't stand any more, so it just shut down. I can't feel love, I can't feel hate, I can't feel peace—I can't feel anything. My emotional self is just gone. It won't open up, because when it does, all the pain and the hurt dashes straight into my heart and breaks it again.

I don't want anybody else to hurt me. I don't want anybody else to get close to me. Because this heart cannot take any more pain, from anything.

When people warn me about the trial, and what's going to happen, I tell them, ''Nothing can hurt me any more in this life than what has already happened.''

I'm not denying that over the next few years, there will be periods in my life when I am going to be back down to ground zero, climbing up from the bottom all over again. That scares the hell out of me, because I've been there before. Sometimes it seems that it's the only thing I have any faith in—that I know I'm in for some more pain.

From the start, there have been people who have encouraged me to tell my story. It never made any sense to me. I knew it would be an incredibly painful process. Mostly, I kept silent, letting others do the talking.

But lately Susan's lawyers have mounted a massive campaign to portray her as a victim, a misunderstood girl who had a lot of hard breaks in her life. Her father committed suicide. Her stepdaddy molested her. As if any of that could explain the monstrosity of what she has done.

Nothing could explain it. I talked to Susan herself, and she couldn't explain it, either.

People look for some magic formula to tell them ''why.'' Why did Michael and Alex, two innocent boys, have to die? They want neat answers. Oh, the woman who did this was mixed up, molested, crazy.

That there's no explanation bothers them. It means that *they* could be living with someone with a dark side who could one day do something unspeakable. It's a hard thought to handle.

But just because what Susan did is beyond all reason doesn't mean she's beyond responsibility. Susan has to pay for what she did.

How do I put my life together from here? What do I do? The past has made me afraid to have another deep relationship with a woman. I'm afraid about having more children someday. What if something happened to them? Even if they were to die in a car accident, or as the result of crib death, how could I handle that? To lose another child would be too much to handle.

I know I'll make it through. I have faith in that, too—that I *will* make it through this. I just know it's not going to be easy. I know I am going to be back down on my knees again, totally at rock bottom again.

I don't often go out to the lake anymore. The last time I went, I watched a single yellow ribbon, unraveled and drifting in the currents by the shore. I had a lot of dark thoughts, suicidal thoughts.

My boys are always in my heart. They give me strength. It's a strange situation for a grown man to depend on two little boys to help him get through each day, but that's the way it is.

Sometimes at night now, I put on ''The Last Song'' and lie on the couch in the dark, remembering them, holding them tight in my mind and my heart.

> *'Cause I never thought I'd lose;*
> *I only thought I'd win.*
> *I never dreamed I'd feel*
> *This fire beneath my skin.*

I can't believe you love me;
I never thought you'd come.
I guess I misjudged love
Between a father and his son.

Michael and Alex, your daddy loves you. Nothing that happens in this world will ever change that.

DEAR MICHAEL AND ALEX: A SELECTION OF LETTERS, POEMS, AND REMEMBRANCES

One important thing that helps me through these dark days is all the cards and letters that I've received. Many are from people who have suffered grievous losses themselves and want to share their experiences and assure me that yes, I can make it through. The sun *will* break through.

These sentiments help during the lonely times when I'm missing my boys. I know that most of the people who sent letters were not really writing me. They were trying to reach out and touch the innocence and goodness of Michael and Alex.

I appreciate every piece of mail I've received as a tribute to my boys. All the generosity, love, and kindness in this world is uplifting, and I will never forget it.

Here are a few selections. I wish I could find space to print more, but I wanted to let people see the incredible good of people all over the country, all over the world.

Dear Mr. Smith,

I am one of three children in my household. I have a nine-year-old sister and a three-year-old brother. I am eleven years old, and I have been watching the case since day one. I had been hoping that Michael and Alex would be found alive. I couldn't stop crying when I found out they were dead. I felt as if they were my brothers. I couldn't imagine being able to stay so calm if it were my brother or sister. I watched your breakdown at your boys' funeral. I felt a little better knowing that Michael and Alex were buried together, in the same casket. I still cry when I see their pictures on TV. My heart goes out to you.

My prayers are with you,
Marnai Boose
Conyers, Georgia

Dear Mr. Smith,

Our minds just can't let go of the tragedy that has come into your life.

But our thoughts and prayers are with you during this time of sorrow and they will be with you during the time of healing that God has for your brokenness.

I wanted to send these snowflakes for this holiday season that will be both hard for you and a time of happy memories.

I am sending one for each of your boys, Michael and Alex, in loving memory and to let you know they have captured the hearts of my husband and me both.

We love you, David, with a special love.

"WHITE AS SNOW"

Their lives were as white as the purest snow.
As pure as the love they came to show.
As gentle as the touch of their tiny hands.
That reach across a heart broke land.
As tender as their kisses to their daddy's face
That reached us all with warmth and grace.
Michael and Alex, two of God's richest blessings
To God's earth, they have blessed us all.

Geraldine Brown
Austin City, Oklahoma

Dear David,

I just wanted to let you know that your little ones are missed and loved dearly by me. As a mother of six (two little boys the same age as Michael and Alex) I think of them every day. My heart aches and my arms feel empty. I cry each day and seek comfort through the Lord and His Holy Spirit.

This senseless tragedy has left me in great pain. When I heard the truth, I dropped to my knees and cried out, "Oh, God! How could this have happened?" The only peace I have is knowing your little angels are now glorified in heaven.

I want you to know that if I can help you in any way, I would like to. I would have sacrificed my own life if I could bring your precious children back. I pray for you and your family daily. For now, I've dedicated my life to God. Seeking His wisdom and trying to please Him all my days. What a joyous day it will be when we are reunited with our God, Michael and Alex!

Karen Hack
Easton, Pennsylvania

"THE ANGEL CAME"

Daddy, don't be hurt and sad no more,
Dry your tears and smile for us.
Alex and I are fine, now on golden shore
In a beautiful land of laughter and loving trust.

We cried and panicked, thinking the worst
In that cold and wet, dark place.
We were pretty scared at first,
'Til we saw the angel's face.

Her touch a soothing, gentle, guiding light,
Her voice was calm and oh, so sweet.
She said, no need to struggle, cry or fight.
She was there to take us both to God, to meet.

We did as we were told.
See? You taught us right.
We just let go our earthly hold
And went to see our Lord that night.

Even angels cry, we saw that day.
They smiled through shining tears,
As they held us in loving ways
To ease our hurts and fears.

God held us too, in arms so big and strong
And rocked us 'til we slept,
He sang a wonderful song,
While the angels softly wept.

God says we're truly home right now,
And we're happy in his loving touch,
But Alex and I want you to know how—
We love you, Daddy—so very, very much.
Love, Michael

Michelle Holliday
Anderson, South Carolina

Dear David Smith,

I am writing you this letter because I just want you to know how much your children mean to me and my family.

I am so sorry that this has happened to you. There isn't a day that goes by that I don't think about your Michael and little Alex.

I have put a newspaper picture of your boys up on top of our entertainment center. I feel like they were a part of me.

From the very first time I saw you and Susan on TV, my heart went out for ya'll. I hoped and prayed that they could catch this guy who had taken the children. I even worried if he was changing Alex's diapers.

I mean, I really did believe Susan. But when I found out otherwise, that it was Susan who did the unthinkable crime, it felt like my heart stopped beating.

I wanted to come to South Carolina so bad, and bring my children with me. My six-year-old said he wanted to touch that water. And my other two children just wanted to see.

But my husband said that it was too far to travel by myself with the kids. One day, I don't know when, the children and I will go there to be even closer to your children.

I just feel like it's something I must do.

Does Susan have any kind of remorse for what she did? I just don't think she'll ever know how much hurt and pain she has caused everyone.

I also ask myself over and over again, why? If she felt like making away with herself, why didn't she just give you those babies?

I mean, she should've known that they would want to be with you because you were a part of them and they were a part of you. I'm just so sorry that it happened this way.

Please forgive me, I hope I'm not hurting you in any way by writing this letter. I'm just trying to make some sense out of all this, and I just can't!

I could not go one day without seeing my children's faces, their sweet little smiles, and those lit-up eyes. I just wish there was something I could do or say to make this hurt go away.

But I don't think that there is. To me this is a hurt that hurts so bad that it stands the test of time. I know it will never be forgotten.

I have watched and taped some of the interviews. And you said that it hasn't touched home plate with you, about the boys being gone.

Well, I'll tell you something. While Christmas draws near, please be stronger than ever, because when you awake this Christmas day, your hurt just might touch that home plate! So may God be with you always and just remember you have got a lot of friends, near and far.

The Haneys
Elmont, Alabama

Dear David,

I am compelled to write to you. I have prayed for you and your beautiful sons Michael and Alexander every day, often many times each day, and always when I wake in the middle of the night, because my thoughts are immediately of you and your broken heart. Like the nation and the world, I have shed many tears for those wonderful children.

I don't really know what the right thing is to say to you. I want you to know that my husband and I, as parents, hurt for you in a manner which is beyond description. I know there are millions of us who wish we could just hug you, somehow absorb some of the pain from your being, share the pain of this horrible burden you must bear for the rest of your life. I thank God that you have a wonderful family and network of friends. Please let them help you all they can. In the final analysis, it is all that anyone can really do.

We watched you speak with Katie Couric, and we were so impressed with your courage and dignity. Your love for your sons just leaps from your face and eyes. At the mention of their names, you somehow are framed by a light. Surely God is trying hard to receive some of your pain. I hope that you can find a way to surrender as much as possible to Him.

Because of your request, I will pray for Susan. I must admit it is very, very difficult, but possible only because you have asked us to. I am not sure of what to pray for on her behalf, so I can only ask God that His will be done. Since none of us truly knows what His will is, we can only trust Him now.

I will close by telling you what lovely angels I perceive Michael and Alexander to be. I am positive they are watching out for you now as you watched out for them. Your suffering will be hard for them to bear because of their obvious love for you. I pray that the joy they brought you in their short lives will somehow sustain you to go on in your life.

Our love to you,
Don and Joyce Frommel
Waikoloa Village, Hawaii

Dec. 8, 1994
David,

   I am a father. Until July 19, I had four children. One girl, 17, named Becky, was married on July 8. I also have three boys, Brian, fifteen, William, eight, and Kevin, twelve, who drowned on July 19. I still have four children—three on earth and one in heaven.

   It was so hot in July and Kevin and William wanted to go swimming. They finally talked their mother into taking them—after supper the three of them went down to the river, which is within walking distance of our house. Kevin was just learning to swim. I stayed at the house to clean out the car, but I went down to the river to get them before going to work. I got there just in time to see Kevin struggling.

   I was the only one who heard his cry for help. I ran into the water clothes and all, even though I could barely swim. The hormones took over. My wife was yelling for help and others came running. When I was about five feet away, he sank beneath the surface, just barely out of reach. In a few seconds, I was also crying for help because of the current. As I went down, somebody grabbed me. They pulled me to shore but they couldn't find Kevin.

   The sheriff brought the rescue team and they searched until after 11 P.M. I thought I would die. The days that followed were almost unbearable. Newspaper reporters and photographers had to be dealt with. I searched the river desperately for my son. Others helped. There was a great outpouring of volunteers with boats, planes and even a helicopter. People were everywhere.

   The town we live in and the town where we go to church were just wonderful, but it got to where I could hardly stand all the attention. When the news of your situation came and they said you had shut yourself in a room, I thought, "Yeah, good for him." I wanted so bad to do that.

   I wrote this not to pour my troubles on you but to let you know I can identify with you in your suffering. The reason I couldn't shut myself in a room is I am a minister. Some think they have answers, but really nobody does. Things just happen.

   David, I want you to know that I care. If you ever need someone to talk to, you can call me. As I said, my heart goes out to you. It aches for you. I will keep praying for you.

   Sometimes it's easier to talk to a stranger. We're walking down the same road of grief and I'm sure you've found, as I have, that life hasn't stopped. In fact, it hasn't even slowed up. You have some hard days ahead. God will give you the strength to make it. Your life will never be the same, but you can find the strength to go on. I hope you didn't take this letter wrong. I want to be a help, David.

God bless you,
Don Eastham
Albany, Oregon

David Smith,

When I finally got around to finishing the card I wanted to send you, I realized I still had a whole lot more than a card's worth of things to say to you, hence the addition of this letter.

I've never done this before—written to some unfortunate soul I learned about through the media, but there's never been a case before that's affected me the way yours has . . . and I dare say I hope there never again will be!

I always suspected *Susan Smith. I'm not sure if that was because of my own cynicism or the fact that I noticed right off that Susan never looked at the camera to which she was speaking. The first time I saw her, I said to my friend who was with me, "There's more to this story and I suspect Susan Smith has more to do with this than she's telling . . . She's lying. She can't look the camera in the eye."*

Nevertheless, I got down on my knees and prayed for those two angels, never knowing it was already too late for that until nine days later. And now that I do know, I've prayed for those two innocent souls, and for you, and for everyone in Michael and Alex's families . . . and even Susan Smith.

My prayers are with you, David, truly. And remember to keep your faith—God did not *do this, Susan did—but God can hasten your healing.*

Sara Hartsfield
Missouri City, Texas

Dear David,

I feel your sorrow as deep as does most of the nation. Like millions of other people, I was stunned and shocked when they announced that Susan had confessed.

I tried for several years to have a child. I lost four. Then God gave me the most beautiful boy. He is the air that I breathe and the reason that the sun rises in the morning; he alone has put the shine in my eyes, the same one I saw in yours when you spoke of the happy times with the boys. They were so beautiful and innocent. They captured the hearts of so many people. I know grown men who wept at the news of their passing. As a mother I cannot understand how or what would push Susan to be prompted to do such a cold and cruel thing. As a parent I can share in a place in my heart the deep sorrow of your loss. I grieve with you and wish you Godspeed.

I need for you to know that each soul that comes into our lives does so for a reason. I know that you may not see this yet, but there are parents all over this nation who are looking at the quality of time and love they give their children due to this terrible thing that has happened to you and your beautiful boys. God gave all of us as parents a shock strong enough to cause us to look at the type of time and love given to our children.

I know that it may be hard to understand or comprehend now, but God knew just what he was doing. He gave your children a very important mission in their short lives. We will all eventually heal and you will become stronger. Believe in God and in yourself. You gave them more love in their short lives than most children receive in a lifetime. Some day you will feel their tender arms around you again and see their sweet, innocent smiles. Someday we will all be together again.

Please feel free to write or call me if I can be of help in any way.

I have faith and I feel that you are a very good person inside who needs some added strength. Your children were sent to this world to achieve a change and they have done just that. I would like to have one of the picture buttons that were made of the children just to remind people in this end of the world that they are still with us in every hug and kiss we give our own.

Deborah Kemp
Garland, Texas

Dear Mr. Smith,

I have no idea if you will even receive this letter, as I have only your name and town for an address. I had to write to you as a parent.

I am the father of two sons who I love very much. My wife and I have been following your story on the news and in the newspaper. No words can express the heartfelt sympathy we extend to you and your family during this terrible time. I can only imagine the torment and grief you are experiencing.

Be certain that there are millions of people with and without children who are praying for you and your family in the hope that sometime soon you can pick up the pieces of your life and go on. None of us can understand the how and why of what has happened. There are so many things that happen in our world that cannot be explained. You can only start fresh and go one with your memories, keeping a small spot in your heart for your sons.

You can be certain that Michael and Alex are with God now and experiencing peace. As time passes, your pain, too, will diminish and you will again be a whole person ready to experience a full and wonderful life.

In sympathy,
David Lawrence
North Canton, Ohio

Dear David,

My wife and I go camping a lot. At night, when all the stars are shining, we always go to the beach and look up at them to see how bright they are. They are all fixed and set in their places, each one of them. Some are faint and some are bright—the ones that are the brightest seem the closest. But the next time we go camping, there will be two new stars that we will see—Michael and Alex. For the Lord said we will shine like the stars, and those two boys are shining in all their glory. Michael and Alex will no doubt be the nearest and the brightest of all, for they are so dear to all our hearts.

David, during the holidays, especially Christmas, try not to think of what we have lost but what God has gained. I lost my brother, and each time I think of him I get a sick, hollow feeling that cannot be filled up. So your hurt will always be there, no matter how long you live, but you have to look at it as if you will be with them again one day. Then all your pain and hurt will have been worth it, for you will see Michael and Alex with God and be able to look upon all three of their faces, and that will be the greatest reward that anyone could ever receive in his lifetime.

David, I don't know if you are getting our cards and letters but I feel we cannot send you enough. We are many miles apart, but I have to let you know how much we really care. I hope that you have found a little comfort from them. If you have, then my intent has not been in vain.

David, I don't want to dwell on the subject, but I sure hope you can find it in your heart to stand by Susan—she needs all your support and more. Whatever we do, we should not hold that kind of hardness in our hearts.

Your friends,
Jim and Gail Hyten
Waterford, Michigan

MICHAEL AND ALEXANDER SMITH

The entire nation looked for you.
We searched and hoped and prayed.
But nothing could have prepared us,
For what we found out that day.

We will never understand this.
We keep asking and asking why,
We wanted so much to find you,
We can't simply say goodbye.

It hurts us all so deeply,
Millions of tears we've cried.
If our love and tears could have spared you,
You never would have died.

The nation fell in love with you.
In death we love you still.
It may take us forever,
For our broken hearts to heal.

Two precious hearts stopped beating.
Four beautiful eyes are at rest.
Jesus has you with him now,
And we know you're with the best.

It broke our hearts to lose you,
But you did not go alone.
A part of us went with you,
When Jesus took you home.

With love,
Carol Sullivan